Dedication

To my wife and editor, Gerianne, a paddling widow,
for all her help and support.

To my daughters, Margaret and Patricia, for all the
paddling we have done and will do.

Acknowledgments

Special thanks to Edison Gardner, owner of Wooden Ski and
Wheel in Plattsburgh, N.Y., Dennis Aprill, Press-Republican
outdoors columnist, Dr. Lawrence Soroka, director of the
Adirondack Experience and Lake Champlain Sea Kayak
Institute at Plattsburgh State University of New York, and
Robert Shea, night editor at the Press-Republican, for their
guidance and constructive criticism.

First Edition

Printed in the United States of America

Trail Marker Books
www.trailmarkerbooks.com

ISBN: 0-9759432-0-0

Front cover photo: The author
on the Saranac River near Picketts Corners

A Trail Marker Books guide to

Kayak and Canoe Paddles in the New York Champlain Valley

15 narrated paddling daytrips
with maps, photographs, directions
and more

By Jack Downs

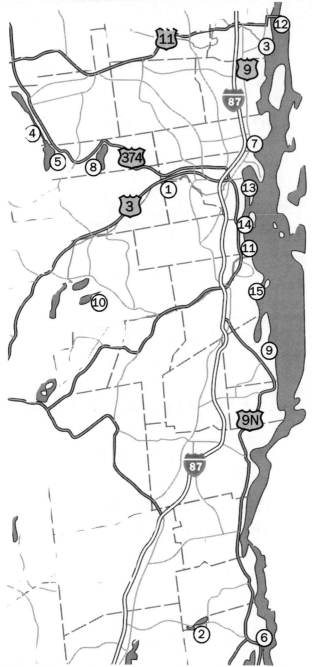

Circled location numbers correspond to numbered paddle chapters.
Chapters are numbered in order of increasing difficulty.

TABLE OF CONTENTS

Photo/Jack Downs

The makings of a perfect paddling day: clear sky and quiet water on Upper Chateaugay Lake.

Introduction

FOREWORD

The lakes, rivers and ponds of the New York side of the Lake Champlain Valley are a paddler's paradise. Both experienced paddlers and newcomers to kayaking and canoeing will find plenty of trips to keep them on the water.

I knew this when I bought my first kayak. But after a few nearby trips on waterways where I have boated frequently I found myself asking: "What next?"

This book is an attempt to answer that question. I have researched and mapped 15 paddling daytrips. Most are possible to complete in a couple of hours. Many can be broadened into daylong adventures. All include variations, side paddles, maps, directions and details.

I hope this book will answer the question "What next?" for you. And better yet, I hope this book will start you discovering your own trips, your own paddling adventures.

ABOUT THIS BOOK

All the distance measurements in this book were calculated using a global positioning satellite (GPS) receiver. Handheld GPS units have become so inexpensive, sophisticated and remarkably precise that many hikers and boaters use the new technology routinely.

With a GPS unit, easily purchased at area outdoors stores or online outlets such as Amazon.com, you can calculate average paddling speed and use that number to estimate the expected duration of a measure paddle. The time taken for paddles in this book is based on my average paddling speed of 3.5 to 4 mph. Your speed will certainly vary from this, making my trip-duration estimates only a rough guideline.

However, you certainly don't need a GPS receiver to enjoy paddling. You can take one of my measured paddles, travel the route, and use the time taken to estimate your average paddling speed.

In addition to GPS information, estimated duration and trip distance, each narrated paddle includes a difficulty rating: easy, moderate, difficult or some combination of these.

Setting these ratings was one my toughest, and most subjective, tasks as an author. Whitewater enthusiasts use a numeric "class" rating that can be quantified. Flatwater paddlers have no such objective scale on which to rate paddles. I have arranged the paddles in numbered chapters beginning with easier trips and ending with harder voyages.

The criteria I used to assign ratings are: wind and wave vulnerability, current, distance from shore, distance from boat launch, distance from assistance and total trip distance.

But changing conditions can, and often do, wreck this rating system.

For example, Eagle Lake easily meets the criteria to be rated as one of the easiest paddles in this book. But, in just the right weather conditions, a really determined wind could find its way between the sheltering mountains, roiling the waters, lashing the west end of the usually peaceful pond with whitecaps, turning a fun family canoe outing into a white-knuckle, teeth-grinding ordeal.

On the other hand, the voyage round Valcour Island is rated as one of the most difficult trips in this book. The open-water paddle across a channel that is known for wind and waves, combined with the isolation of the east side of the island, make this a trip that should only be attempted by more experienced paddlers. But paddle this route during a dead calm and it is just as safe as the Saranac River.

One environmental factor that doesn't figure into my ratings is water temperature. It's natural to push the season, paddling as early in the spring and as late in the fall as you can. But cold water kills. Spring trips, when the air temperature can be deceptively warm, are especially dangerous. Before you get in your kayak or canoe, ask yourself how you would feel swimming.

ABOUT KAYAKS

You do not need a super-expensive high-tech kayak to have great fun on the water and complete the trips described here. On the other hand, don't purchase a kayak at a department store or a buying club.

Although this book is not a guide to buying kayaks, I do have a bit of advice: paddle before you buy. One person's dream kayak is another person's dud. And if you've never kayaked before, don't worry. Kayak dealers should be willing to orient new paddlers and give them the tools they need to make a buying decision.

Another option is to rent kayaks, gaining experience in a number of different boats. You will learn how different style kayaks handle while you pick up paddling experience.

Finally, when it comes time to buy a kayak, don't hesitate to spend a bit more for a comfortable seat or a kayak that is a few pounds lighter.

Hopefully, you will spend hours and hours in that kayak seat. Spending an extra $50 or $100 here is a good investment. And you only have to hoist that kayak onto your car a few times to understand the value in 10 pounds less weight.

ABOUT CANOES

I have paddled many miles in canoes over the years. I like canoes. But I love kayaks.

Canoes are the station wagons or family vans of small boats. If you have a lot of people or gear to carry, canoes are for you.

All the trips described in this book can be paddled in both canoes and kayaks. That said, let me caution that, especially in the open-water Lake Champlain paddles, canoes are more influenced by the wind and more vulnerable to waves than kayaks. Extra caution should be taken when planning an open-lake crossing in a canoe.

But that's not the real reason for my prejudice. For me,

kayaks can be a fitness tool – like cross-country skis or a mountain bike. But canoes are a method of transportation, a vehicle. And because canoes are harder to handle solo – on the water and in the parking lot – canoe trips usually become expeditions, with all the planning that a multi-person voyage requires. But with a kayak I can decide to take an afternoon paddle and be on the water 30 minutes later with little planning.

Of course there are exceptions. There are kayaks that are too big and heavy for a paddler to handle alone. And there are modern solo canoes that bear little resemblance to the 16-foot aluminum behemoths that I paddled as a child.

MY KAYAK

So what do I paddle?

All the trips in this book were paddled with a recreational touring kayak, a Wilderness Systems Pungo Superlight. The Pungo, a proven design common in rental fleets, is not stylish. But it is great for me: light, simple and safe.

Some of these paddles were also completed with a Wilderness Systems Pamlico two-person kayak in which I often paddle with my two young daughters.

To be realistic, I intentionally wanted to complete these trips in an entry-level kayak, a solid step-up from a department-store kayak, but well below the sticker price of a top-of-the-line sea kayak.

I don't endorse any kayak model or manufacturer; there are dozens of great boats out there. Modern recreational kayaks are lighter, safer, cheaper and better equipped than ever before.

SAFETY AND CONVENIENCE

This is not a manual on kayak and canoe safety. There are clubs, camps, colleges and shops that offer boating safety courses, advice and books. I strongly suggest you take a class before heading out on the water. You must be able to rescue yourself and others in the event of a mishap. In the New York Champlain Valley region, a great place to start is Plattsburgh State's Adirondack Experience: http://www.plattsburgh.edu/academics/adx/

Although I don't review safety equipment and techniques in this book, I do have some basic advice.

The absolute most important safety device is your life jacket. WEAR YOUR LIFE JACKET AT ALL TIMES.

Photo/Jack Downs

A life jacket is critical for safety. A good hat, plenty of water and appropriate footwear add comfort.

There is no excuse, in a canoe or kayak, to paddle without a flotation device.

Because of this, I suggest that you spend the extra money to get a really good, really comfortable life jacket. And try the jacket on sitting in your kayak. A bulky, awkward vest will ruin your boating experience or, worse yet, make it more likely that you remove the protection while paddling.

The second most important piece of safety equipment is your brain. Use your senses. Analyze what you see. When conditions are changing, when wind picks up, when waves come in unexpectedly, don't be afraid to turn back or find shelter.

It is right about here that safety guides usually say: never paddle alone. I have to be honest. If I never paddled alone, I'd almost never get on the water. So, whether you paddle in a group or alone, make sure someone responsible knows where you've gone, when you expect to be back, and what they should do if you are overdue. It's also a good idea to leave a note in your car with this information.

There is much more that can be written about safety. But, as I said, this is not a safety manual. However, on the topic of convenience, my experience on these paddles has taught me a few items that might be helpful to beginner paddlers:

--Always bring sunscreen, bug repellent and a couple of water bottles.

-- Get a really good hat. Ideally, your hat should be fastened to your shirt or life jacket. When the weather turns windy you won't want to circle back through waves for a sinking hat.

-- In a dry bag, pack a towel. The most versatile tool, a towel can be a pillow, bandage, seat cushion and so much more.

PADDLING WITH KIDS

Although canoeing and kayaking can be fun outdoor activities for the whole family, you'll need a special approach to help kids enjoy their time on the water.

For example, if you are a hard-core paddler you may look forward to hours of open-water exercise, meditating with the rhythm of the paddle strokes, soaking up the scenic vistas, the ever-changing scene of light, shadow and water. On the other hand, you are crazy if you expect a 6-year-old to sit quietly in the bottom of a canoe for 20 minutes – let alone an hour – while you paddle along in the blazing sun.

Want to avoid the tears, yelling, sulking and recriminations? I can't make any promises. But here, from my own experience and mistakes, are a few tips for paddling with kids.

Don't let life jackets be a problem. Cheap children's personal flotation devices (PFDs) are horrible. Look at your kids in those big bulky orange things, pinching at the neck, pulling at the belly. Are you surprised that they are miserable?

Good life jackets are expensive, but they are worth it. Bring your kids to the kayak store. Let them try on jackets, sit in kayaks and take ownership of the buying decision. You won't have to beg for them to put on their PFDs before your next paddling trip.

In addition to being more durable, quality life jackets are very adjustable. Many children fit well into small-adult sized PFDs. They will be able to use these jackets for many years.

But don't rely completely on life jackets. Kids need swim lessons and should be able to handle themselves in the water before heading out on canoe or kayak trips. It

Photo/Gerianne Wright

The author and his children in a two-person kayak adapted for three.

is also a good idea to have kids practice swimming and floating in their life jackets, just so they know what it feels like if they ever end up in the water.

One last thing about PFDs: Don't give in. Even in a good life jacket your kids may complain. They will want to take it off because it's too hot, because it's just a short trip, because you're almost back to the launch or because so-and-so doesn't have to wear one. The rule should be inflexible for you and for your kids: everyone in a canoe or kayak must wear a life jacket at all times.

Kids have special needs. Kids get hot, cold, tired, bored and have to go to the bathroom. And all these things can happen in the first 10 minutes. With kids, you need luggage: a book, a toy, extra water, extra snacks, towels for shade. Be creative. But no, I wouldn't bring a VCR and TV.

Adjust your goals; be flexible. I have to admit, this is the part that gives me the most trouble: ditching the trip and spending an hour playing in a stream inlet instead of reaching the rocky point that was my goal.

For example, imagine you've been waiting all week to paddle with your kids, planning an epic Valcour Island circumnavigation. Really, paddling across the channel and spending the rest of the afternoon exploring a beach and playing in the sand would be a great success. Be prepared to stop, explore, play and change your plans.

If your paddle is going wrong and there is no beach nearby, find a sheltered spot and swim beside the kayaks. Leave your life jackets on and practice rescue techniques.

Kids want control. Another way of putting this is, "Kids want to paddle."

We want to protect our kids, and we want them to be independent. This eternal struggle follows us from home and school onto lakes and rivers.

Obviously, very young children will have to sit in the bottom of the boat as passengers. Bring an extra paddle, let them try it a bit. They will get tired, bored and give up, hopefully before they smash their fingers against the gunwales. Don't consider this a failure. This is how learning begins.

For some kids, the next step will be paddling tandem in a canoe or two-person kayak. I hope this works better for you than for me. At least in kayaks, I have found that the teamwork needed to synch strokes may be too much to ask.

Instead, I have been gratified to see how quickly my young children have picked up paddling alone in their own kayaks, especially if the boat is sized properly. Depending on the child's level of physical and emotional maturity, you could start them at 8 or 10-years-old.

It makes sense, really. Paddling tandem, the child doesn't feel the impact of the stroke. Paddling is a chore, an exercise. They know the adult is just humoring them; that the adult will take over.

Instead, put a child in an appropriately sized kayak with an appropriately sized paddle and they immediately feel the impact, the necessity of each stroke. Paddle along in your own boat, bringing a tow line. Unsure if your child is ready? Rent a second kayak for the day and give it a try.

Of course, I'm not suggesting you send an 8-year-old off on her own unsupervised. And don't plan a long trip or go anywhere that could be scary. Your child's first solo paddles will probably be little more than 15 minutes of play and circles while you float nearby, followed up with an hour on the beach and a snack for positive reinforcement. If your child goes too far or tires too quickly, just hook on the tow rope and take over.

What about older kids? Most of my experience, and therefore my advice, concerns younger children. Older kids who aren't attracted to kayaking and canoeing for the simple pleasures of outdoor exercise may need other incentives. Fishing and camping from canoes and kayaks adds a whole new dimension to the experience.

With the proper training and equipment older kids may want to branch out into whitewater or racing.

Eventually, it seems, many kids become more attracted to powerboats, water-skiing and personal water craft.

This is an investment in a future when you will paddle longer and longer trips together. You are introducing your youngster to an outdoors experience that will hopefully lead to a lifetime of healthy outdoors adventure.

WARNING AND DISCLAIMER

This book is designed to inform canoers and kayakers about possible paddling trips in the New York portion of the Lake Champlain Valley. This is not a safety manual, boating instruction manual or a guide to boat shopping.

All readers must understand that canoeing and kayaking bring with them risks. All readers should attend boating safety classes and canoe/kayak paddling classes before attempting any of these trips. However, be informed that even with proper training and equipment accidents can result in loss, injury or death.

The author has attempted to make this guide complete and accurate. However, there may be mistakes or omissions, both typographic and in content. Therefore, this text should be used only as a general guide. Furthermore, please understand that this book contains information that was correct at the time of writing but that may become obsolete after the printing date.

The author and publisher shall have no liability or responsibility for damage, loss, injury or death caused or alleged to have been caused directly or indirectly by information contained in this book.

If you do not wish to be bound by this warning and disclaimer please return this book to the publisher for a full refund.

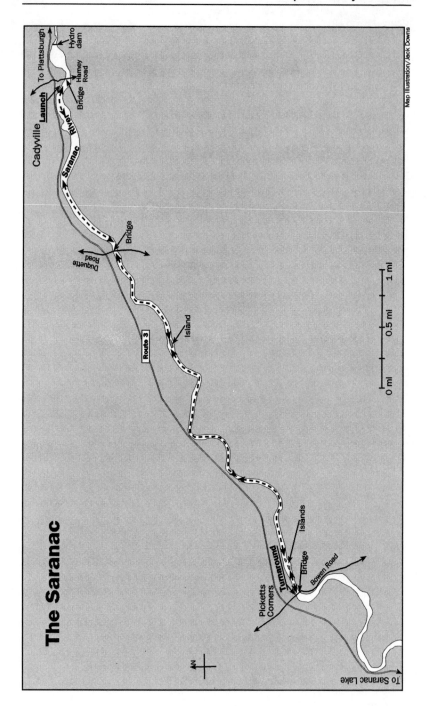

The Saranac

The Saranac
Cadyville to Picketts
Corners

A Paddle for All Levels on a Sheltered, Slow-Moving River

NARRATIVE

A paddle on the Saranac from Cadyville to Picketts Corners is a tale of two shores.

The south shore: meditative and wild. Long stretches of steep banks, cedar swamp and abandoned meadow with seldom a house or road in sight.

The north shore: back yards, Route 3 traffic noise, disused camps, junked vehicles with occasional, welcome stretches of undeveloped forest.

However, this civilized/uncivilized contrast doesn't extend to the river itself. From Cadyville to Picketts Corners the Saranac is a restrained river, tamed by a NYSEG hydropower dam. Even a determined west wind can do little more than create ripples on the well-sheltered water. Unless the water level is low – as it can be in times

Photo/Gerianne Wright

The Saranac near Picketts Corners.

TRIP STATS
Rating: Easy to moderate
Cadyville beach to Picketts Corners: 6.25 miles
Round trip: 12.5 miles
Total time: 3.5 to 4.5 hours
Launch GPS location: N44-41.778, W073-38.168
Launch type: Sandy beach
Facilities at launch: None
Wind: Sheltered from most mild and moderate winds

of drought or dam maintenance – the current is barely noticeable. You won't find any white water here.

The combination of sheltered water, slow current, sandy-beach access and surprisingly sparse boating traffic make this an especially good family paddle.

On the other hand, with a possible round trip of more than 12 miles, and ample isolated scenery, there is plenty here to attract paddlers of higher skills who are looking for a few quiet hours of waterborne exercise.

This paddle begins at the Plattsburgh Town Beach in Cadyville. During beach season, avoid the swimming area. Here the river is at its widest, pooling just upstream from the Harney Road Bridge. This first stretch of the trip, broad and exposed, is the only place the wind can be more than a minor annoyance.

Paddle upstream from the beach: almost due west. After about 0.6 miles the river turns to the north, narrows, and quickly loses its pond-like feeling. At about 0.75 miles a large mud bank with a marshy top protrudes from the south shore. When the water is high, this bank – a favorite haunt of herons – becomes an island. Follow the north shore (right while going upstream) to avoid the muddy shallows.

At about 1.1 miles the river again swings to the south, completing one of many snaking turns in a generally westward course. Here, a stream enters from the north, creating a small sandbar. This is the outlet from Gougeville Springs, part of the Town of Plattsburgh water system. You may see people on the road here, filling bottles with spring water at a public-access pipe.

The river passes under the Duquette Road Bridge at about 1.85 miles. Upstream from here is my favorite part of the Saranac. The river winds away from Route 3, motorboats are rare and development falls away. An island approaches at about 3 miles; it is navigable on either side. Herons, ducks and geese ply these waters. If you are lucky, you may catch sight of a beaver near the shore, or a family of white-tailed deer coming down for a drink.

The south shore, often steep and forested, gradually gives way to abandoned meadow and brush-choked lowlands. The north shore is sometimes populated, sometimes farmland.

At 4 miles into the trip, and again at 4.6 miles the river touches Route 3, only to turn sharply away.

At 5.75 miles two small islands appear. Here, especially in times of low water, the current will begin to become noticeable. Some determined paddling might be necessary where the islands narrow the stream. Pass both these islands on the south (left side while going upstream) reaching the Bowen Road Bridge, just adjacent to Picketts Corners, at 6.25 miles. Here, a small concrete pad serves as a launch and pullout spot.

An ambitious paddler may try to pass under the bridge. Although the river is navigable for a few hundred yards more, it is not worth the effort. The currents under the bridge are swirling and strange. The stream gains speed upstream and quickly becomes shallow.

The return from the Picketts Corners Bridge is by no means repetitive. Sure, this is the same river. But, to adapt the old saying, you can't put your paddle in the same river twice. Even this slow-moving section of the Saranac is ever changing. I've also noticed that return trips never feel the same as the trip out. The wind shifts, the light changes, the wildlife moves and the river offers up something new with every turn.

Don't expect your downstream 6.25 miles to be much faster than the upstream trip. The mild current may not do much more than compensate for the natural slowdown after a couple hours of paddling. On the return trip I am also more likely to daydream, follow a duck family, glide and snack or explore stream inlets and islands. Return to the Cadyville Town Beach at 12.5 miles.

The Saranac, civilized and wild, brings me back again and again.

SIDE TRIPS/VARIATIONS

-- A trip to the New York State Electric and Gas hydropower dam, a paddle of only a couple hundred yards, makes an interesting start or finish to a longer paddle on the river. However, because you must respect and respond to the danger signs near the dam, I don't suggest this side paddle for novice boaters.

From the Plattsburgh Town Beach in Cadyville turn to the east and paddle under the Harney Road Bridge. You will pass some rock ledges that may seem geologically out of place.

Here the river pools just before passing over the dam, one of several hydropower barriers on the river. Follow the south shore and beware of the dam. If you pull out on

the south shore a short distance from the dam and look
over into the chasm below, the ledges you saw at the
Harney Road Bridge make more sense, matching with
the falls and the rapids below.

-- Of course, this trip may be shortened by turning
back anywhere along the route. Another option is to turn
this into a one-way downstream trip, paddling with
friends. Park a car at the Cadyville end, and then drive to
Pickets Corners, beginning the trip at the Bowen Road
Bridge and ending at the Cadyville Town Beach.

DRIVING DIRECTIONS

From the east: From Plattsburgh, take Route 3 west.
The launch will be about 1 mile from the intersection of
Routes 3 and 374. Staying on Route 3, look for the turn to
the Cadyville Town Beach just past the intersection of
Route 3 and the Harney Road, visible on the left. The
turnaround spot for this paddle is another 5.7 miles west
on Route 3. To reach it from the east, look for the Pickets
Corners sign; turn left onto the Bowen Road. Park in the
small lot just before the bridge.

From the west: Take Route 3 east. You will pass a sign
for the hamlet of Redford. The intersection of Route 3 and
Bowen Road – the upstream turnaround point for this
paddle – is about 3.3 miles ahead. See directions above.
The launch for this paddle is at the Cadyville Town Park,
about 5.7 miles further to the east. Watch for the beach on
your right. If you get to the intersection of Routes 3 and
374, you've gone to far.

TRIP NOTES

Eagle Lake

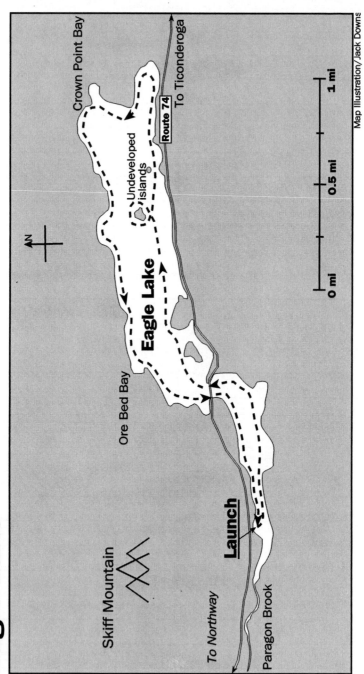

Map Illustration/Jack Downs

Eagle Lake
A Circumnavigation

An Adirondack Pond with Islands to Explore

NARRATIVE

The southwestern slopes of the Adirondacks, watershed for Lake Champlain, are dotted with lakes and ponds perfect for kayaking and canoeing.

Of these, Eagle Lake is one of my favorites – a great spot for family paddling. A cliff-sided clear-water Adirondack pond, Eagle Lake runs east-west, making it largely immune to all but a strong west wind. Better yet, the lake passes under a low highway bridge, and includes two unposted islands, numerous bays and inlets for exploring.

This paddle begins at the state fishing access off the south side of Route 74 about midway between Ticonderoga and Route 87. Although the parking area may be cramped on busy days, the launch is great for small boats.

Eagle Lake is composed of two lobes. This launch is in

Photo/Gerianne Wright

Near the Eagle Lake inlet, not far from the boat launch.

TRIP STATS
Rating: Easy to moderate
Total distance: 5 miles
Approximate trip time: 1.5-2 hours
Launch GPS Location: N43-52.438, W073-36.297
Launch type: Sandy state boat launch
Facilities at launch: None
Wind Exposure: Sheltered from all but strong west wind

---

the west corner of the southwest lobe, a portion of the lake that is at no more than a quarter the size of the main body to the northeast.

Beginning here you quickly leave any boat-launch hustle and bustle behind. This lake's character asserts itself immediately: steep cliff sides, deep water and discreet lakeshore camps. A pair of loons fish nearby and, if you get lucky, maybe you'll even see one of the lake's namesakes floating overhead.

Paddle to the east, approaching the Route 74 bridge at a little less than a mile into the trip. There is just enough headroom here for a kayaker to cruise through without ducking. Pass into the main lobe of the lake.

From here the lake turns again to the east, passing a large island and a point developed with camps and homes, some apparently old Adirondack structures. Central to the east end of the lake is a large rocky island. Approach it gliding over a marked milfoil bed, a hazard to motorboats but barely noticeable in a kayak or canoe, reaching the unnamed and uninhabited island at 1.6 miles.

A loop around this cliff-sided but heavily eroded island shows no posted signs. There is a crude landing on

Photo/Gerianne Wright
The author approaches the Eagle Lake boat launch.

the east side, with just enough room for a canoe or kayak to be carefully lodged. Explore the island and you will find the rock foundation of a long-ago structure. A companion to this island is a much smaller outcropping – little more than a boulder with a bit of vegetation – to the southeast.

This smaller, exposed rock island is a nice spot to pull out and sunbathe. However, here the pond borders on

Route 74, and a steady stream of noisy log trucks headed to the Ticonderoga paper mill may become an annoyance.

Beginning an eastward course again after a ring around the island, now at 1.92 miles, skirt the edge of the second, smaller island and head for the deep bay at the southeast extreme of the lake, reaching it at 2.5 miles. Development here on Route 74 is heavier. Now turn to the north and west, leaving the highway and following the shore to the more rugged, less developed north side. Return to the Route 74 bridge at 4.4 miles, passing under and continuing to the launch, finishing the paddle at 5 miles.

SIDE TRIPS/VARIATIONS

-- Exploring the islands and inlets of this small lake can add hours to this short paddle.

-- For family or novice paddlers who want an extremely sheltered and controlled trip, stay in the small lobe of the lake, paddling and exploring, perhaps going as far as the highway bridge, playing echoes underneath.

DRIVING DIRECTIONS

Coming from the north or south, get off the Northway at the Ticonderoga Exit 28. Now on Route 74, follow the signs for Ticonderoga. The turn for the launch is about 8 miles ahead on the right. The small state sign reads "Eagle Pond Fishing Access."

TRIP NOTES

TRIP NOTES

_____

_____

_____

_____

_____

_____

_____

_____

_____

_____

_____

_____

_____

_____

_____

_____

_____

_____

_____

_____

_____

_____

_____

_____

_____

_____

_____

The Great Chazy

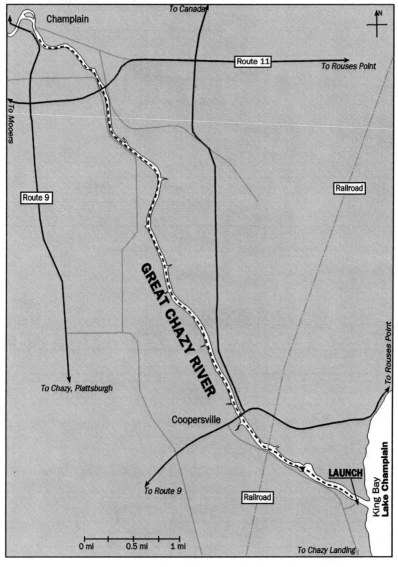

The Great Chazy
To Champlain and back

A Great Paddle for a Tranquil Day

NARRATIVE

With its formidable name, is the Great Chazy River truly great, wonderful, fantastic? No. A more fitting label for the segment of stream between Champlain and the river's mouth might be the Passive Chazy, Serene Chazy or Tranquil Chazy River.

But if you are an experienced kayaker looking for a reprieve from Lake Champlain's wind and waves, or a novice paddler who needs a quiet stretch of water to build confidence, this trip could be great for you.

Of course, the Great Chazy River's name comes from its size and length, which is truly great when compared with the Little Chazy River to the south, which is truly small. North and west of Champlain, the Great Chazy divides into numerous branches, twisting and turning, often little more than a large stream, covering most of northern Clinton County, even reaching its namesake, Chazy Lake.

Photo/Gerianne Wright

Small marinas dot the shore near the Great Chazy River
boat launch.

TRIP STATS
Rating: Easy to moderate
Total distance: 8.8 miles
Approximate trip time: 2.5 to 3 hours
Launch GPS Location: N44-55.928, W073-23.196
Launch type: Concrete boat launch, free
Facilities at launch: Rest rooms
Wind Exposure: Relatively sheltered, exposed to
strong south wind

However, in its last gasp, running through the flat farm country to Lake Champlain, the Great Chazy becomes a wide, slow, dark, canal-like river, popular for fishing and small marinas.

We begin this paddle at a state boat launch at the mouth of the Great Chazy River on Lake Shore Road in Coopersville. There are no beach options for launch here. You must use the large concrete launch, better suited for powerboats.

Turn upstream, paddling northwest, the river gradually turning more northwards. This first mile of the river is popular with boaters, so be watchful for traffic and wakes. Several small marinas and many homes and camps dot the shore.

Pass under an old railroad bridge at 1 mile. This line is active, so don't be startled by the occasional train thumping overhead. Pass under the Route 9B bridge at 1.32 miles. By 2 miles into the trip, camps, docks and houses are rare. Farmland, cows and cornfields replace these features. The riverbanks become somewhat overgrown, a few snags protruding into the water.

Remarkably, the river has narrowed very little. And still, the current is very slow. In fact, if a south wind is

Photo/Gerianne Wright
The Great Chazy is a quiet, agricultural river. Much of the shoreline is forested and undeveloped.

blowing down on the lake, the breeze that makes it through the tree-lined shores may more than counteract the downstream current. The river twists and turns very little here, bearing almost directly northwest. Herons and ducks are common along this stretch. Keep an eye out for kingfishers and, basking in the sun on logs at the river's edge, the occasional turtle, some quite large.

At 3.1 miles, the river makes one of its few sweeping turns, to the west and then back to the north, and the vista opens, the forested banks now giving way to low farmland and pasture. At 4 miles, as you approach another bend, passing a large New Holland farm equipment dealership on the west bank, a bridge becomes visible ahead.

This is the Route 11 highway bridge at 4.4 miles, a good place to stop and turn downstream. Here the river narrows dramatically, snaking through the Village of Champlain, making its transition to a more stream-like character. With the gentle help of the current, begin the paddle back to Lake Champlain.

Although the pasture bordering this upstream section of the Great Chazy is private land, none is posted. If you need to stretch your legs, do it here. Closer to the lake the riverbanks are steep and the water is deeper.

Paddling downstream, watching the river grow at first wilder, trees crowding the shores, and then more developed with camps, docks and homes, I am reminded how rivers change minute by minute. Changing light, current and wind make the downstream paddle a new experience, a new river.

Pass under the Route 9B highway bridge at 7.46 miles and the CP Rail span at 7.84 miles. Return to boat launch at 8.8 miles.

SIDE PADDLES/VARIATIONS

-- For family paddlers who want an abbreviated trip or anyone who is pressed for time, simply shorten this trip by turning back sooner. However, don't expect the downstream current to cut the time of your return dramatically. The current here is so slow that a south wind of any strength can actually make the downstream paddle longer than the upstream portion.

-- If the wind is calm or coming from the west, follow the river downstream into King Bay. You will see a narrow, carefully marked boating channel. Kayaks and canoes have much more freedom here, and there are marshes and inlets to explore and plenty of birds to watch. The deep bay is bounded on the northeast by Point au Fer.

DRIVING DIRECTIONS

Access for this paddle is reached from Lake Shore Road in Coopersville. To get there, begin on Route 9. Drive to the intersection of Routes 9 and 9B, about 19 miles north of Plattsburgh and 3 miles south of Champlain.

Take Route 9B heading east toward Coopersville. Watch for Lake Shore Road, about 2.8 miles after this turn. If you cross the green bridge over the Great Chazy you know you've gone too far. Turn on to Lake Shore Road heading south. The boat launch is about 1.3 miles ahead on the left.

TRIP NOTES

_____

_____

_____

_____

_____

_____

_____

_____

_____

_____

_____

_____

_____

_____

_____

_____

_____

_____

_____

_____

_____

_____

_____

_____

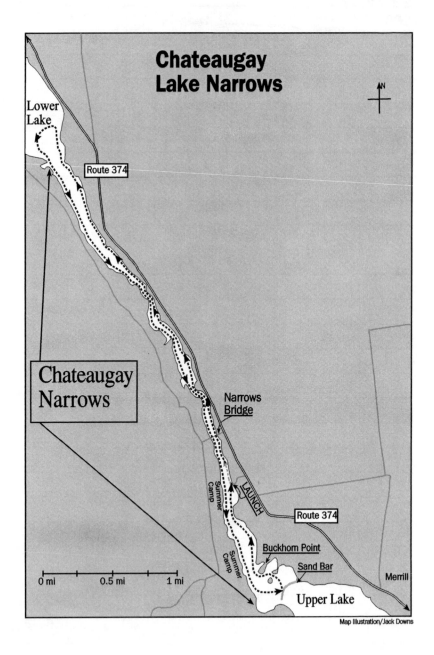

Chateaugay Lake Narrows

Lower Lake

Route 374

Chateaugay Narrows

Narrows Bridge

Summer Camp

LAUNCH

Summer Camp

Route 374

Buckhorn Point

Sand Bar

Merrill

Upper Lake

0 mi   0.5 mi   1 mi

Map Illustration/Jack Downs

Chateaugay Lake
The Narrows

A Sheltered Paddle to a Sandbar Beach

NARRATIVE

I had to ask myself, before writing about this paddle: "Do I really want to tell people about my lake?" You see, Chateaugay Lake is my home lake. I've spent at least some of every summer of my life here. But, thinking about the question, I came to two conclusions:

First, my lake is no secret. A state boat launch brings in plenty of motorboat traffic. Second, the best thing for a lake is more paddlers. Kayakers and canoers respect the water, put little or no stress on wildlife and help keep motorboaters in line.

So, it is with a clear conscience that I recommend Chateaugay Lake. The narrows, described here, make an excellent family paddle. The Upper Lake, described in another chapter, has enough distance, wind and waves to satisfy experienced paddlers.

We begin this paddle at a boat launch on the Chateaugay Lake Narrows, one of the few bits of truly

Photo/Gerianne Wright

The author with kids in the kayak paddles south on the
Chateaugay Lake Narrows. The rocky point ahead is Buck
Horn. Lyon Mountain looms in the background.

TRIP STATS
Rating: Easy to moderate
Total distance: 7 miles
Approximate trip time: 2-2.5 miles
Launch GPS Location: N44 46.416, W073 58.810
Launch type: Concrete boat launch, free. Small beach
launch area nearby.
Facilities at launch: Rest rooms
Wind Exposure: Protected from most wind.

public land on this waterway. Although the launch is a traditional state-run ramp — large and concrete — you will find a small, sandy beach just to the south that may be better suited to canoes and kayaks.

If you are one of those people who like to eat dessert first, you'll want to turn south and paddle directly to the "Sandbar," the simple one-word description for the jewel of Chateaugay Lake, a quasi-public beach that separates the Narrows from Upper Chateaugay Lake. Find a description of the route from the launch to the Sandbar near the end of this narrative.

But because mom always taught me to eat my meat and potatoes before my pudding, I start this paddle turning north and passing under the Narrows Bridge at .46 miles. Immediately, the Narrows narrow and become river-like. At 0.7 miles the waterway sweeps to the west, beginning a series of winding turns, passing a small inlet at 0.9 miles into the trip.

Both shores here are populated. The east shore (left), following Route 374, is a carpet of cottages, camps and homes. Although this is not a wilderness paddle, it is a friendly waterway: kids fishing off docks wave as you pass; motorboats are slowed by the careful navigation; near-tame ducks swim along looking for handouts or sit sunning on docks; herons fish in the marshes on the west bank.

After about 2 miles of paddling, Lower Chateaugay Lake begins to open ahead. The shoreline here is lower and the vista opens to low mountain ridges in the distance and the broader water ahead. The next .75 miles of northwards paddling takes you through the wide, regular channel that leads into this broad, oval-shaped lower lake. If the wind allows, you will reach the grassy sandbar point on the west shore that marks the beginning of Lower Chateaugay Lake at about 2.75 miles.

Turning south to begin the return trip here, the bulging form of Lyon Mountain begins to dominate the landscape, occasionally hidden by the forested shorelines as the Narrows twist and turn.

After passing under the Narrows Bridge at 5 miles, stay to the right, paddling along the west shore and passing the boat launch at 5.45 miles. Just a short distance north of the launch, also on the west shore, you will see the waterfront activity area of one of the lake's three children's summer camps, Camp Jean D'Arc. During the camping season, the area can be busy with boats, so paddle carefully, giving the camp swimming area a wide berth. Here the lake widens briefly.

Indeed, the next mile – the stretch from the launch to the Sandbar – is the busiest on the lake. Stay near the west shore and out of the central channel; watch for wakes. At 5.9 miles pass a second large kids camp, Camp Chateaugay, directly across from Buck Horn Point, a sharp rocky point that extends from the east shore, narrowing the lake.

As you pass Buckhorn, watching for boat traffic, cut across the channel and make for an island to the east. Pass on either side of this small island, just bigger than the large camp it holds, reaching a sandy beach at 6.2 miles.

This is the Sandbar: A long, sandy finger that nearly cuts the lake in two, half exposed and half a shallows that is impossible for motorboats to cross. By tradition, boats dock on the Narrows side of the bar and swimmers use the Upper Lake side of the peninsula. A tiny, deep-water channel is marked where the Sandbar nearly touches Bluff Point.

Whether the Sandbar is your destination for a day of family beach play or merely a rest stop before a more ambitious paddle into the Upper Lake, be respectful of the swimming area and don't trespass onto private property where the bar joins the mainland.

When you are ready to leave the Sandbar and return to the boat launch, stay close to Buck Horn Point to avoid traffic. Follow the east (right) shore back to the boat launch, ending the trip at 7 miles.

SIDE TRIPS/VARIATIONS

-- For a shorter paddle, simply leave the boat launch, head south (left) and travel 1 mile to the Sandbar.

-- You may want to extend this trip with a paddle through Lower Chateaugay Lake, a long oval without many shoreline features until you reach the Forge Dam at the lake's extreme northwest end.

-- For more information about paddling Upper Chateaugay Lake, see the next narrative.

DRIVING DIRECTIONS

The only public access to Chateaugay Lake is a state boat launch in the Narrows. Reach it from Route 374 between Lyon Mountain and Chateaugay.

Coming from the east, the boat launch driveway is about 5.5 miles from the intersection of Route 374 and Standish Road in the hamlet of Lyon Mountain. If you reach the Hollywood Inn, you've gone a bit too far.

Coming from the west, the boat launch driveway is about 12 miles from the intersection of Routes 374 and 11 in Chateaugay. Watch for the Hollywood Inn. The boat launch is your next right.

TRIP NOTES

_____

_____

_____

_____

_____

_____

_____

_____

_____

_____

_____

_____

_____

_____

TRIP NOTES

Upper Chateaugay Lake

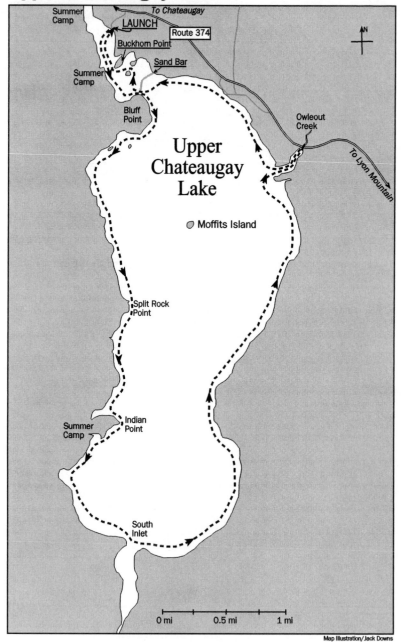

Summer Camp

To Chateaugay

LAUNCH

Route 374

Buckhorn Point

Sand Bar

Summer Camp

Bluff Point

Owleout Creek

Upper Chateaugay Lake

To Lyon Mountain

Moffits Island

Split Rock Point

Summer Camp

Indian Point

South Inlet

0 mi   0.5 mi   1 mi

Map Illustration/Jack Downs

Upper Chateaugay Lake
A Circumnavigation

A Bigger, Wilder Paddle

NARRATIVE

This is the other face of Chateaugay Lake. The Narrows is sheltered and safe. But the Upper Lake is a wilder, bigger paddle. At 10 miles, this circumnavigation boasts enough size and variety to interest even experienced paddlers for an afternoon.

This trip starts at the Sandbar, the semi-public beach that is a nearly complete barrier between the Chateaugay Lake Narrows and Upper Chateaugay Lake. For directions to the launch site, and from the launch to the Sandbar, see the narrative for the Chateaugay Lake Narrows paddle.

Begin this paddle at the narrow channel between the southern tip of the Sandbar and Bluff Point. From here follow the shore to the south (right). After about 0.25 miles the vista opens around Bluff Point displaying the bulk of this big lake: points and bays ahead, rocky

Photo/Jack Downs

Standing on the Upper Lake side of the Sand Bar looking to
the southwest, the beach sweeps away to the left, is covered
with shallow water, and ends at a deep-water channel that
connects the Upper Lake and Narrows.

TRIP STATS
Rating: Moderate to difficult
Total distance: 10 miles
Approximate trip time: 3-4 hours
Start GPS Location: Chateaugay Lake Sandbar
N 44-45.825, W073-58.461
Wind Exposure: Exposed to a variety of winds.

shoreline, Lyon Mountain rising over the distant eastern shore and Moffitt Island in the center. However, the southern lobe of this lake, including the South Inlet, is hidden from view.

The shore here is all private, much of it posted. Pass two small islands tucked in near the shore, really just huge boulders with a few trees. With care, you can navigate the water between these islands and the shore, but it's easier to pass them on the open side.

At 0.87 miles pass the ruins of a grand hotel, lost to fire. All that remain are the stone chimneys, standing silent in the lakeside forest. Before the automobile changed vacation patterns, Chateaugay Lake was home to a number of these luxury lodges. Wealthy city-dwellers would arrive via train and stagecoach, trading heat and disease for the Adirondack summer.

Just past these ruins you'll see a sand beach that is roped off as a swimming area for one of the lake's three large children's summer camps. The wealthy city-dwellers may not come for summer-long Adirondack vacations any longer, but many of the same families now send their children off for a similar experience.

Avoid the swimming area and the water-ski instruction powerboats that are common in this part of the lake. Follow the shore, now turning to the southeast, and paddle past large summer homes. Round a stone jetty and rocky headland at 1.95 miles into the trip.

This is Split Rock Point. Passing it opens the southern, quieter end of Upper Chateaugay Lake, with views to the South Inlet and mountain vistas beyond. You may see loons here, herons in the marsh ahead, and swimming beaver in the evenings or early mornings. Split Rock Point also marks the end of road access to this western shore. To reach camps between here and the South Inlet you must hike in or travel by boat.

At 2.58 miles pass an older camp adorned with strange and spooky natural sculptures. At 2.92 reach the tip of a dramatic point that shoots out of a deep and narrow bay. This last protrusion before the South Inlet is named Indian Point. In season you may see a large teepee here, one of several buildings that house a wilderness children's summer camp.

From here, paddle through the last bay before the South Inlet, past a startlingly bright red house that is part of the children's camp. But don't get too close to the shoreline as it grows lower and becomes marshy. The water shallows here. Reach the South Inlet, where Middle Kiln Brook flows into Upper Chateaugay Lake at 4.2 miles.

The inlet is broad and river-like here at the lake. Although the brook shallows and narrows upstream, it is navigable by kayak or canoe for some distance. For this measured trip, however, we will pass the mouth of the inlet and stop for a break at a narrow sandy beach just to the east, the odometer reading 4.64 miles.

Photo/Jack Downs

The view north from near the southern end of Upper
Chateaugay Lake.

From here you can explore the edge of the marsh or rest on the sand and admire this little-traveled end of the lake. Pinched by Indian Point, the southern end of Upper Chateaugay Lake looks bowl-like from this perspective. One caution: being this close to the South Inlet wetlands, be sure to bring your bug repellent.

Back on the water, paddle north up the east side of the lake. Camps become visible a short distance from the South Inlet here. Pass the blunt point opposite Indian Point at 5.87 miles into the trip, leaving the southern end of the lake. Ahead, Moffitt Island appears to be almost dead on, looking deceptively close to the western shore. In fact, the island sits almost dead center in the northern lobe of the Upper Lake. On a quiet day a trip around the island makes for a pleasant open-water paddle. Unfortunately, Moffitt Island is posted private property.

At 7.2 miles reach the extreme northeastern corner of the lake. The shore again turns low and marshy, marking the mouth of Separator Brook. From marsh the shore changes to sandy shallows and beach. On a warm day without the nuisance of a south wind this spot would make an interesting explore on foot.

Heading now almost directly to the north, at about 7.7 miles into the trip, watch on the right for the entrance to Owlyout Creek. Enter the inlet at 7.85 miles, a large log-cabin style camp on the left and rocky point on the right. Head for the power lines visible straight ahead. Threading your way through the channel may be difficult if the water is low. Scoot under the Route 374 highway bridge and arrive at the Owlyout Tavern, a bar and restaurant, at about 8.26 miles.

You may want to take a break in the tavern, or an explore up Owlyout Creek. When you're done, trace your route back through the Owlyout inlet and, after reaching the lake, strike out to the northwest, heading along the shore toward the Sandbar.

At about 9.5 miles the shoreline turns to sandy beach, all posted. Look to the south and you'll see the entire Upper Lake in one large panoramic vista: Lyon Mountain on the left, Moffitt Island in the center, South Inlet far to the rear, Indian, Split Rock and Bluff points to the right.

This stretch from the Owlyout to the Sandbar is also where you will be most vulnerable to a south wind and the rolling waves it can rile.

At 10 miles, now sheltered by Bluff Point, return to the channel that marks the division of the Narrows and Upper Lake.

SIDE TRIPS/VARIATIONS

-- Exploring the South Inlet can add a significant time and distance to this trip. But be sure to bring your bug repellent.

-- The Owlyout Tavern, described in this narrative, is one of three bar/restaurants accessible by boat on Chateaugay Lake. The others are the Hollywood Inn, which is on the Narrows, adjacent to the boat launch, and the Lakesider, near the northeastern corner of Lower Chateaugay Lake. Stringing all these into a day on the lake would certainly earn an ambitious paddler his breakfast, lunch and dinner.

DRIVING DIRECTIONS

Use driving/launch directions for the Chateaugay Lake Narrows paddle.

TRIP NOTES

TRIP NOTES

Ticonderoga

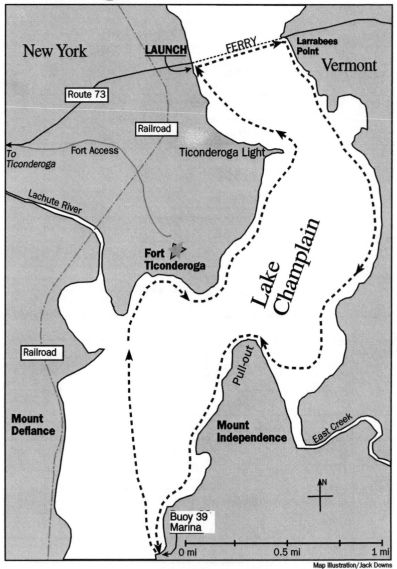

Map Illustration/Jack Downs

Ticonderoga
An Historic Paddle

Ticonderoga Ferry to Buoy 39 Marina, with Views of the Fort

NARRATIVE

Thousands of people visit Fort Ticonderoga every year. I doubt a tenth that many paddle the historic watercourse below.

Standing on Fort Ticonderoga's battlements, browsing its exhibits, tourists learn that the structure was founded by the French to fight the British in the 1750s. Battles were fought here through the American Revolution when the fort protected a nascent nation threatened by British invasion from the north.

A paddle in the river-like Lake Champlain below the fort teaches a different kind of lesson. Follow the water and you feel, in a visceral way, the strategic value of this short stretch of lake. Many brave soldiers and sailors gave their lives defending and attacking the fortifications

Photo/Gerianne Wright
The author paddles west across Lake Champlain from the Ticonderoga boat launch, heading toward the ferry landing on the Vermont side.

TRIP STATS
Rating: Moderate to difficult
Total distance: 6.3 miles
Approximate trip time: 2 to 2.5 hours
Launch GPS Location: N43-51.213, W073-23.130
Launch type: Public boat launch with concrete ramp
Facilities at launch: Rest rooms
Wind Exposure: Moderate exposure to south wind

---

on these shores, threading this same channel. This is truly a paddle through history.

This trip begins at the Ticonderoga Boat Launch, a free state launch adjacent to the Ticonderoga Ferry.

Paddle parallel to the ferry path, bearing almost directly east, and traverse the lake here, a crossing of just less than 0.5 miles. A glance at the ferry reveals that this is not the normal Lake Champlain commuter boat. The Ticonderoga vessel is an old-fashioned cable ferry, well suited to this narrow crossing.

Now on the Vermont side, bear south, following the shore and heading toward a rounded and steep-sided headland dead ahead. This is Mount Independence, counterpoint to the blunter promontory where Fort Ticonderoga stands just across the narrowing channel. The fort is still invisible to the paddler here.

Hundreds of years ago, smaller fortresses stood several places along this stretch, including a formidable one on Mount Independence. Even a kayak — if such a vessel ever touched these waters before the 1900s — could not have passed these battlements unchallenged.

As you paddle this 1.75-mile stretch from the east end of the ferry line — Larabee's Point — to Mount

Independence, especially if you paddle late in the summer, you'll notice another characteristic of this southern tip of Lake Champlain: milfoil weed beds.

The shallows here are sometimes chock full of this invasive nuisance weed. Although the growth is a lesser problem for canoes and kayaks than for motorboats, skirt the denser beds or you'll be pulling strands of weed off your paddle after every stroke.

Reaching the tip of Mount Independence at 2.2 miles, having passed a number of small bays and one broad marshy inlet, you'll find a rock ledge sheltered from the south wind that makes a convenient but slippery pullout.

Mount Independence is a Vermont-managed historic site. If you explore these heights you will find trails and interpretive signs explaining the peninsula's military history.

As you round Mount Independence, the restored Fort Ticonderoga with its distinctive gray battlements and red roofs becomes visible directly across the channel. But still, the view is obscured. Instead, as you continue to paddle south along the Vermont shore, look to the rugged New York shoreline where Mount Defiance dominates the view.

Still paddling the Vermont shore, sheltered from the sometimes-annoying south wind, continue south to Buoy 39 Marina at 3.3 miles into the trip. This is a good spot to take a break and, looking to the north, survey Fort Ticonderoga.

From here, by crossing the channel in a slanting northwest direction, then turning north to head directly toward the fort, you can paddle with the historic structure slowly looming larger and larger, reaching the shore at the base of the fort at 4.65 miles. The property here is all posted. Paddle east along the cliff that defends the foot of the fort, rounding the headline at 4.9 miles.

As you begin to turn to the northeast, heading toward Ticonderoga light, a navigation marker on a rock breakwater, beware of a submerged barrier, perhaps the derelict remains of an abandoned breakwater, just to the north of this point. On this stretch the view is farmland away on the north and east with Mount Independence passing away on the east.

Reaching the Ticonderoga light at 5.7 miles into the trip, the view changes dramatically. Now you can see the cable ferry passing back and forth, a somewhat broader stretch of lake beyond, and well to the north the smokestacks of the huge International Paper Mill, a reminder that for much of its human history Lake Champlain was more important for commerce, transportation and industry than for scenery and tourism.

You'll find a sandy beach on the north side of the Ticonderoga light. However, the property is posted. From here it is only a short paddle back to the Ticonderoga Boat Launch, ending the trip at 6.3 miles.

SIDE TRIPS/VARIATIONS

-- North from the Ticonderoga Ferry the lake widens slightly, passes International Paper Mill in the west shore just before Five Mile Point — about 5 miles from the ferry — cuts in from the Vermont shore, pinching the lake narrow again.

-- Continuing south from Buoy 39 Marina the lake briefly continues to narrow and become more river-like, reaching one of its narrowest spots in this stretch about 2.5 miles below the marina at Vermont's Chipman Point.

-- After your paddle, why not take a few hours to tour Fort Ticonderoga. Standing on the battlements with the rest of the tourists, looking down on the lake below, you can have the satisfaction of knowing that you paddled the water most visitors only gaze on.

-- If a south wind keeps you off Lake Champlain, try a paddle on nearby Eagle Lake. This east-west lake is cliff-sided and sheltered from all but the strongest winds. The paddle is described in another chapter of this book.

DRIVING DIRECTIONS

Coming from the north or south, get off the Northway at Exit 28. Now on Route 74, follow the frequent signs to Fort Ticonderoga and Ticonderoga Ferry. The launch is on Route 74, about 1.3 miles past the intersection where Routes 74 and 22 diverge. Look for it on the right only a few dozen yards before the ferry landing. From the Northway to the boat launch is about 21 miles.

TRIP NOTES

_____

_____

_____

_____

_____

_____

_____

_____

_____

_____

TRIP NOTES

Point au Roche

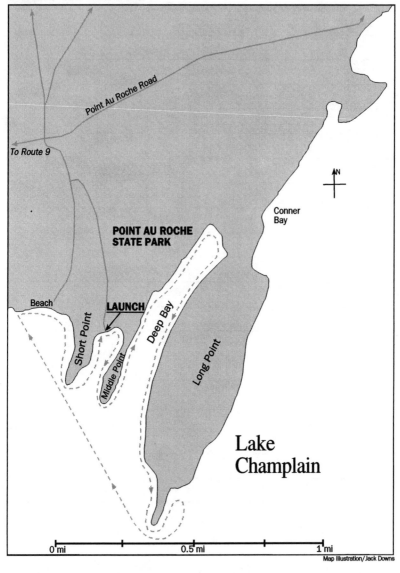

Point Au Roche Road

To Route 9

N

Conner
Bay

**POINT AU ROCHE
STATE PARK**

Beach

LAUNCH

Short Point

Deep Bay

Middle Point

Long Point

Lake
Champlain

0 mi   0.5 mi   1 mi

Map Illustration/Jack Downs

Point au Roche
Bays and Points

Exploring the intricate shoreline
of a popular state park

NARRATIVE

Long before the state park was founded, Point au Roche held a certain magic that brought people here.

First, native tribes and early settlers made this their home. Later, Point au Roche became home to farms, a children's camp and a short-lived theme park called Fantasy Kingdom. All that is gone now. What remains is the magic: finger-like rocky points, deep and forested bays, and a long stretch of sandy beach on Lake Champlain.

This paddle begins at a recently built state boat launch within Point au Roche State Park. During the summer season you will be charged a day-use fee at the park entrance. The traditional concrete launch is flanked by rocky beach. I prefer to launch from the beach area just to

Photo/Jack Downs

The arms of Middle Point (left) and Long Point reach around Deep Bay, pinching it to a narrow opening at the center of the frame.

TRIP STATS
Rating: Easy to moderate
Total distance: 4 miles
Approximate trip time: 1.5 hours
Launch GPS Location: N44-46.449, W073-23.228
Launch type: Both traditional concrete launch and rocky beach. A parking fee is charged.
Facilities at launch: Rest rooms
Wind Exposure: Bays are sheltered. Paddling near the points is exposed to winds from the south and southwest.

---

the west (right when facing the lake) of the ramp.

This is Middle Bay. It is bound by Short Point on the west and Middle Point on the east. First paddle a short distance to the northeast to reach the base of Middle Bay, gradually turning to the southwest, following the shoreline of Middle Point toward the open lake.

Quickly, the landscape and geology of Point au Roche assert themselves: narrow, cedar-topped points extending into the lake, sided with ledge and broken rock. Middle Point is the narrowest of the park's three points.

Paddle to the tip of Middle Point, avoiding the rocky jumble that extends some way into the lake from the eroded and undercut point, reach the apex and turn to the northeast at 0.4 miles, beginning to follow the east shore of Middle Point into Deep Bay.

This bay truly is deep, bounded by Middle Point and Long Point. Although you may be exposed to wind and waves as the bay begins, only a strong southwest wind can reach vary far into this sheltered water. During the summer season you may have to thread your way through moored sailboats taking advantage of this quiet resting place. On the points you may see hikers traveling the walking trails that parallel these shores.

Reach the deepest part of Deep Bay at 1.2 miles into the trip. Follow the shoreline around the bay's curved base and turn to the southwest again, paddling along the west shore of Long Point, heading toward the open lake once more. At 1.4 miles pass a dock and pumpout station that services moorings here.

Unlike the other points, Long Point is broad and large. Connected to the mainland by a narrow neck, this point feels like an island. And like most Lake Champlain islands, its southern end rises into a rocky headland. But this point has an unusual feature. At about 2 miles into the paddle the point narrows abruptly and casts a rocky finger far out into the lake. The bay here shallows: beware of rocks near the surface as you round this southern tip of Long Point at 2.3 miles.

Here, the vista opens: Vermont and the hazy Green Mountains away to the east; a wide swath of the Adirondacks to the south and west. However, if there is much wind blowing you may not have time to enjoy it. You are exposed to wind and waves here.

After a brief loop to peek around the west side of Long Point, turn to the north, aiming for the large rock outcropping just to the west of the sandy beach and brown park buildings beyond Short Point. This open-lake paddle of about a mile through Treadwell Bay will take you past the open mouths of the bays you have explored. However, if the wind is blowing and waves become a problem you may instead want to paddle a short distance into the bays for shelter.

Passing Deep Bay and then Middle Bay provides an

overall picture that contrasts with the close-up examination that came earlier. Reach the rocky outcropping that divides St. Armand Beach at about 3.3 miles into the paddle. Turn to the west and coast past the beach. Reward yourself with a break here, resting on the sand, swimming or strolling in the picnic area.

Avoiding the swimming area during the summer season, continue to paddle eastward along the shoreline, heading toward Short Point. Round the point at 3.8 miles and return to the boat launch at 4 miles.

VARIATIONS AND SIDE TRIPS

-- Extend this trip by continuing down the rugged east shore of Long Point, perhaps paddling through Conner Bay and rounding an unusually shaped rocky headland called Rams Head into Mooney Bay, where a marina marks the border of the State Park. The distance from the tip of Long Point to Mooney Bay is about 2.75 miles.

-- For a shorter additional paddle, from the State Park beach, continue around Treadwell Bay to the west, paddling past a wildlife area and, as you leave the park, homes and camps.

-- After returning to the launch, drive back to Point au Roche Road, leave the park turning to the right, and reenter the park about 0.6 miles to the east at the Nature Center entrance. Here you'll find another parking area, an interpretive center and access to miles of walking trails.

DRIVING DIRECTIONS

Point au Roche State Park is on Point au Roche Road, which intersects Route 9 in the Town of Beekmantown, south of Chazy and north of the City of Plattsburgh.

From the north, drive south on Route 9. Watch for the

intersection with Spellman Road, which provides access to Exit 40 on the Adirondack Northway (Route 87). Point au Roche Road is 0.4 miles ahead on the left.

From the south, drive north on Route 9. Point au Roche Road is on the right, 3.7 miles north of the large intersection where Cumberland Head and Moffitt roads cross Route 9. This intersection provides access to Exit 39 on the Adirondack Northway (Route 87).

Once on Point au Roche Road, watch for the park on the right after 1.6 miles. Enter the park here. During the summer season you will have to stop at the entrance booth and pay a parking fee. Follow the signs for the boat launch. The access road from Point au Roche Road to the launch is 0.8 miles.

TRIP NOTES

_____

_____

_____

_____

_____

_____

_____

_____

_____

_____

_____

_____

_____

TRIP NOTES

_____

_____

_____

_____

_____

_____

_____

_____

_____

_____

_____

_____

_____

_____

_____

_____

_____

_____

_____

_____

_____

_____

_____

_____

Chazy Lake

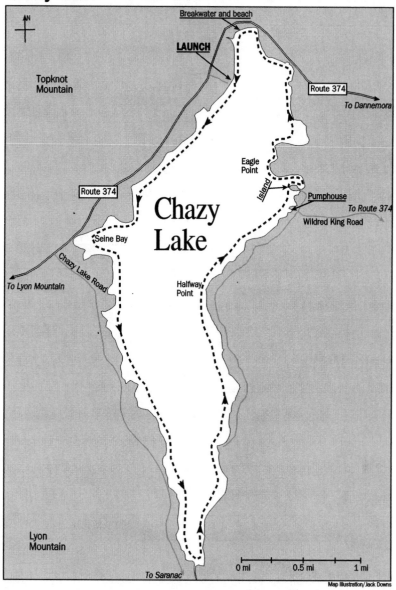

Map Illustration/Jack Downs

Chazy Lake
A Circumnavigation

A Small Lake with a Big Lake Feeling

NARRATIVE

The closest most people get to Chazy Lake is Route 374. The highway snakes around the north tip of the lake and then parallels the shore for a distance before shooting off to Lyon Mountain. Drivers see a fair-sized rounded puddle of a lake, not much more than a large pond.

But paddlers earn a truer perspective. More than half of Chazy Lake is hidden to the south, where a wilderness inlet feeds this surprisingly large body of water.

Starting at the launch, a short distance southwest of the dam that encloses the north end of the lake, paddle to the south and west, beginning a counterclockwise circumnavigation. If you meet wind and waves when leaving the sheltered launch be prepared to turn back and paddle another day. This lake is vulnerable to wind.

The first two miles are heavily populated: a mix of

Photo/Jack Downs
The view from Chazy Lake beach, just off Route 374 and a
short distance from the boat launch.

TRIP STATS
Rating: Moderate to difficult
Total distance: 9.5 miles
Approximate trip time: 3 to 3.5 hours
Launch GPS Location: N44-46.135, W073-48.717
Launch type: Small, free state-run concrete launch.
Facilities at launch: Rest rooms during summer
Wind Exposure: Exposed to a variety of winds,
especially southwest.

summer cabins and homes. The shoreline – a series of small bays and points – is edged with rounded rocks. There are few beaches here.

The view is dominated by Lyon Mountain, a massive mound of a peak in the southwest. If the weather is clear you may spy the fire tower perched on the rocky summit. To the south is Johnson Mountain with Dannemora Mountain off to the east.

At 1.3 miles enter a deep bay with a sandy base. A bit further, at 1.6 miles into the trip, enter Seine Bay, the largest and most sheltered cove on the lake. Here the lake again touches Route 374. I travel only about halfway into Seine Bay, saving my energy for the many miles of paddling ahead.

Leaving Seine Bay about 2 miles into the trip, the shoreline turns more directly south, becoming wilder and more rugged. At about 2.5 miles the water shallows and the bottom becomes sandy, staying this way for about another 2 miles, the result of runoff from streams that race down Lyon Mountain. There are pockets of camps and homes here, accessed from the Chazy Lake Road, including some new construction that nearly reaches the lake's southern tip.

At 2.85 miles pass a bay with a rocky jumble near its base – nearly an island – in which a birdhouse stands on a pole. Pass a birch-covered island, almost touching the shore, at 3 miles. The Chazy Lake Road touches the lakeshore at 3.75 miles. This sandy spot appears to be an informal put-in and beach. However, the shore is posted.

The wild south end of the lake opens at 3.9 miles, leading to the southern inlet at 4.4 miles. The lake is much narrower here and the water covers many barely submerged stumps, some quite large. Paddle with caution.

The Chazy Lake inlet begins as a broad stream. In high water it can be paddled for some distance. In the spring and early summer, make sure to bring bug repellent.

I leave this explore for another day, turning north and continuing the circumnavigation. This is the wilderness shore of Chazy Lake, forested and rocky. Topknot and Ellenburg mountains rise on the horizon in the north. Civilization returns with camps and homes, first sparse, then quickly more concentrated, at 5.25 miles. There is an unposted sandy beach a short way past the first camp you reach here on the west side of the lake: a good place to stop and stretch your legs.

Here, the forested shore turns to birch and cedar, and then completely to birch for about 2 miles. Chazy Lake is known for its loons. You will likely see a pair fishing in this wilder half of the lake, or hear their scolding cry. At 6.5 miles round a large blunt point, an older log cabin and log boathouse near the shore. This is Halfway Point, almost directly opposite Seine Bay. Ahead, the northern end of the lake opens.

Photo/Jack Downs

The quiet south end of Chazy Lake, not far from the mountain stream that is the lake's source.

The open waters between Halfway Point and Seine Bay are a witness to tragedy. A famous drowning here July 3, 1927 killed five students on a school outing, decimating the tiny Dannemora High School senior class. The teacher barely survived, her body and boat washed into Seine Bay by the sudden summer storm.

The party in two rowing skiffs, perhaps overloaded, had tried to cross the lake from Halfway Point heading toward the Lyon Mountain shore. But upon leaving the shelter of the point they were hit by the full force of the southwest wind. One boat made it across. The fatal vessel swamped trying to turn back. For an excellent account of this tragedy and other history of the lake, check out Rod Bigelow's Web page: http://bigelowsociety.com/slic/chazylk.htm

With this somber lesson in mind, thankful for my lifevest, I continue the circumnavigation, the shoreline now veering away to the northeast. At 7 miles enter a large bay with a striking stone building at its base. This is the Pumphouse, the water supply for the Village of Dannemora and the large prison there. A small beach and boat launch here are a second public access to the lake. If a south wind keeps you off the lake, you may want to launch here for a shorter paddle instead. See the variations section below for more description.

Just to the north of the Pumphouse is one of Chazy Lake's claims to fame, a huge stone and timber mansion.

This island retreat was built by Reginald Werrenrath, a popular baritone of the early 1900s, at a time when the famous and wealthy summered nearby in lakeside grand hotels. The hotels are all gone, but the mansion remains. Recently, it was purchased by someone of more modern fame, actress Brooke Shields, who lived here briefly with her mother. However, it has since changed hands again.

Paddle to the causeway that connects the island to the shore at about 7.5 miles into this trip. Round the island and paddle into the deep bay to the north, admiring the architecture of the massive main building and the gorgeous boathouse.

Continue to the north, rounding a rocky peninsula at 8 miles. This is Eagle Point, the last significant protrusion of the lakeshore. Jumbled boulders extend out from the point, and the water here is rock-filled and shallow. This point shelters a large, low-sided bay. Paddle through this bay, heading toward the cement storm wall that barricades the north end of the lake, reaching it at 8.8 miles.

Just to the west is a small town beach and picnic area. At 9.2 miles pass the outflow of the lake. This is the start of the Great Chazy River. Many miles to the north and east this water reaches Lake Champlain. Return to the boat launch at 9.5 miles.

SIDE TRIPS AND VARIATIONS

-- If you are looking for a shorter paddle, or if the wind is from the south, you may want to launch at the Pumphouse. This sandy launch and informal parking spot is off the Wilfred King Road (what used to be called the Pumphouse Road), which leaves Route 374 about 2.9 miles to the east of the Chazy Lake Boat Launch driveway. The Pumphouse and launch area are obvious about 2.2 miles down this road.

-- To expand this trip by at least a mile, fully explore Seine Bay, the lake's south inlet and the deep bays around Eagle Point.

-- While at Chazy Lake, why not combine a hike up

Lyon Mountain with your paddle? To reach the trailhead, drive west about 2 miles from the boat launch driveway to Chazy Lake Road. Take this road about 1.7 miles, watching for a dirt road on the right. Take this seasonal road to an obvious parking area. The trail begins at the south edge of this clearing. Although the trail is unmarked and unmaintained, it is popular and well worn. The trail rises about 1,790 feet in 2.5 miles to reach the 3,845-foot summit.

DRIVING DIRECTIONS

The Chazy Lake Boat Launch is on Route 374 between the Village of Dannemora and hamlet of Lyon Mountain. From the east, the driveway for the launch is about 2.9 miles from the intersection of the Wilfred King Road (formerly called Pumphouse Road). From the west, the launch entrance is about 2 miles past the turn for Chazy Lake Road.

TRIP NOTES

_____

_____

_____

_____

_____

_____

_____

_____

_____

_____

TRIP NOTES

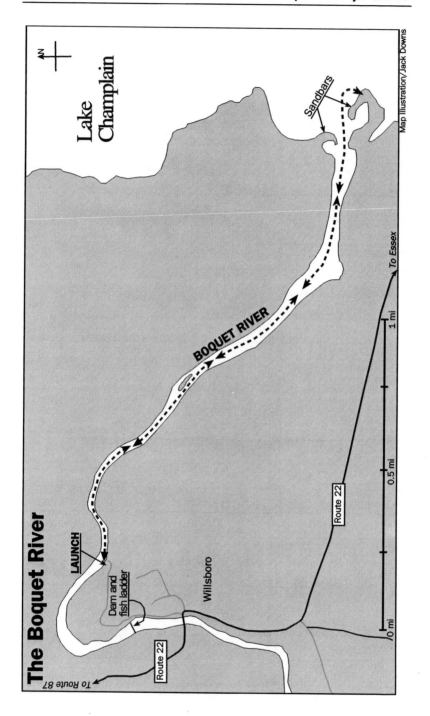

The Boquet River

Lake Champlain

N

BOQUET RIVER

Sandbars

LAUNCH

Dam and
fish ladder

Willsboro

Route 22

Route 22

To Route 87

To Essex

0 mi   0.5 mi   1 mi

Map Illustration/Jack Downs

Boquet River
Willsboro to Lake
Champlain

A Secluded Paddle to a Lakeshore Sandbar

NARRATIVE

Popular with birders, suitable for families, the Boquet River from Willsboro to Lake Champlain is a rare combination of quiet, isolation and adventure.

Starting as a ledge-banked rocky river, transforming into a shallow sandy-bottomed paddle to a gorgeous sandbar delta, this short stretch of river offers wilderness, wildlife and a sense of exploration surprising for its ease and length.

First, a word of caution about rivers in general, and the Boquet in particular. Avoid river paddles after heavy rains or during spring runoff. This placid stretch of the Boquet can become dangerous during heavy flow. In fact,

Photo/Jack Downs
The Boquet River is narrow and quiet at the boat launch. The river widens but stays slow further downstream.

TRIP STATS
Rating: Easy to moderate
Total distance: 4 miles
Approximate trip time: 1.5 hours
Launch GPS Location: N44-22.069, W073-23.175
Launch type: Free concrete and gravel launch
Facilities at launch: None
Wind Exposure: Quite sheltered. Possible exposure to very strong winds.

because the Boquet drains a vast area and begins far into the High Peaks its flow may be more weather dependent than other rivers described in this book.

Begin this paddle at a public, but unmarked small-boat launch just a short distance from the bustle of Willsboro's small downtown. The steep gravel launch is a bit narrow and clumsy, so be careful. From here, let the gentle current take you to the southeast. Eroded gray stone ledges bank the heavily forested shores.

This gentle current is the swiftest you will encounter on this trip. You'll need to paddle to make any but the slowest headway. And it doesn't take much of a south breeze to counteract the current.

The river makes a moderately sharp bend to the east, and back to the south, establishing the southeast direction it will keep most of the way to the lake. Within the first half-mile the rocky ledge and rock-strewn bottom give way to grassy banks and sand bottom, quite shallow in some places.

Reach a small island at 0.7 miles. Stay to the south (right) side of the island. The opposite shore is choked with snags. This little island might be a fun explore for kids.

For the next mile the river is quite shallow. During a dry summer or fall there may be places where a heavily laden canoe or kayak runs aground, making it necessary to get out and haul. But the bottom here is good sand, making the footing firm.

This is a good stretch to practice reading the water. Watch for sandbars, stay to the outside of bends in the river, avoid the center of the wider stretches and guess where the deepest channel will be. Throughout the downstream trip you'll notice that the north bank (left) is posted. However, the south bank is unposted. There are plenty of places to stop, pull out and stretch your legs. However, with the water so low, you may simply stop midstream and step out into the water.

At about 1.3 miles the river narrows slightly and changes character, the shore, now heavily forested with hardwoods, squeezing in from the south. The water deepens slightly and stays deeper through to the lake.

Here, the river's history begins to make more sense. Through the early 1700s, heavy commercial traffic plied these waters. Farms, mines and industry in Willsboro and the surrounding countryside used the Boquet to move products to Lake Champlain and, then on heavier craft, to cities along the lake, Montreal and New York City. Heavy barges carried loads from the mouth to just upstream from our boat launch.

Sadly, generations of heavy use, industry and erosion left the river shallow, silted and less and less valuable for navigation. In the early 1800s attempts were made to reopen the river, but nothing succeeded for long. Eventually, railroads and highways made commercial

Photo/Jack Downs

This hook-shaped sandbar reaches into Lake Champlain at the mouth of the Boquet River.

river travel obsolete.

Approaching the lake at 1.5 miles into the trip, the horizon begins to open. The riverbanks turn to sandy delta at about 1.75 miles, with Vermont's Green Mountains, and the great lopsided profile of Mount Mansfield, visible in the distance on a clear day.

The mouth of the river is flanked by two large, hook-shaped sandbars. The bar on the south shore (right approaching from upstream) is especially large and intricately curved, nearly cutting off a small, sheltered lagoon from the lake. Wind and waves allowing, paddle through the mouth, turning to the south and beaching on the lakeside of this hooked sandbar arm 2 miles into the trip.

Roaming these bars you'll find plenty to explore. Shore birds congregate here, sometimes in vast numbers. The bar is filled with animal tracks. Hawks float above on the lake winds. Herons wade in the marshy shallows. Or maybe you just want to relax on the red-brown sand, having a snack and watching the waves out on the unprotected lake. Willsboro Point is visible to the northwest, the Four Brothers islands directly north and the Vermont shore away to the east.

Beginning the upstream paddle, you may notice the slightest tug of a current. If you are lucky enough to have a bit of a southeast wind blowing from the lake, the current will be more than neutralized. Again, after the first 0.75 mile, as the river shallows, practice reading the water to avoid being caught in the shallows.

Perhaps paddling slower, without the urgency of reaching the mouth and the anticipation of the sandbar, this is a good time to do some nature watching. On a sunny afternoon, the bleached logs that extend into the lake here may be lined with turtles. At first, they are hard to see, but as you pass you'll hear the characteristic "plop" as the wary beasts drop surprisingly fast into the water. Also watch for signs of beaver, active along the shoreline, and for deer peering out from the forest.

Just as you approach the last, sharper river bends before the boat launch, the banks and river bottom becoming rocky, the wooded shores now turning to cedar and pine, the current will become more noticeable. And the stiffest current will be within sight of the launch, only a hundred yards from the trip's end. Unless you've made the mistake of taking this trip after a heavy rain or during spring runoff, this current will still be quite manageable.

Return to the launch and finish the trip at 4 miles.

SIDE TRIPS/VARIATIONS

-- If you are still up for a bit of paddling after returning to the launch, continue upstream. The river is navigable for about 0.3 miles further. Here, you may pull out and explore the ledges and rapids on foot.

-- A number of paddles are possible from the mouth. The true tip of Willsboro Point is about 7 miles north. Whallon Bay and Split Rock Point are about the same distance to the south. Although these destinations may be a bit too far for a casual afternoon's paddle, there are plenty of rocky bays and ledges to explore along the way.

-- For the ambitious paddler, an open lake crossing to the protected Meach Cove boat launch in Vermont is about 4 miles.

DRIVING DIRECTIONS

From Exit 33 on the Adirondack Northway (Route 87) follow the signs to Willsboro, taking Route 22. You'll stay

on this road for about 8 miles. Route 22 takes a turn and
sharp downhill to cross the Boquet River. Immediately
after this bridge turn left onto School Street, the launch is
about 0.5 miles ahead. Pass the Willsboro Fishway and
the Willsboro Wastewater Treatment Plant. The road
turns to gravel and ends in a turnaround and parking
area at the launch.

TRIP NOTES

TRIP NOTES

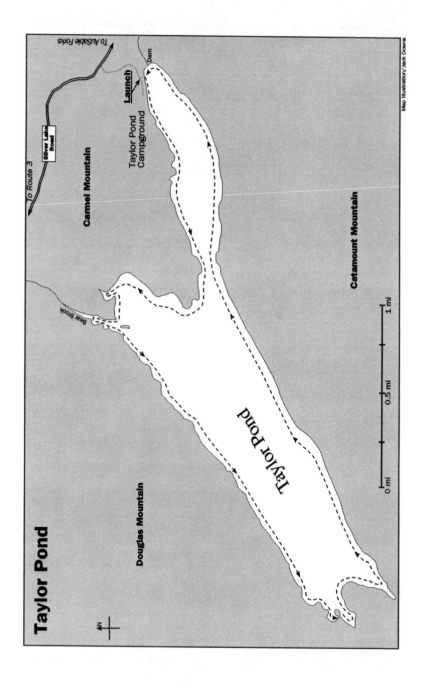

Taylor Pond
A Circumnavigation

A Pond that Paddles Much Bigger than it Looks

NARRATIVE

It is easy to be deceived by Taylor Pond. First comes the name, which carries an air of the safe, the commonplace, the small.

Then the pond's location – a state-managed campground not far from two heavily traveled regional routes – suggests that it is yet another drive-in, have a swim, bring a picnic kind of place: the kind of puddle where you might float on an inflated armchair instead of a kayak.

Don't be fooled. Taylor Pond is really a mountain lake; wilder, bigger and more remote than you expect. In quiet weather, the lake is suitable for novice paddlers. But at the launch you'll see a sign: "Warning: Weather subject to severe change." Take this sign seriously.

Photo/Jack Downs

The Taylor Pond boat launch on a quiet autumn day. This elongated channel leads to the main body of the pond.

TRIP STATS
Rating: Easy to moderate
Total distance: 8.5 miles
Approximate trip time: 3 to 3.5 hours
Launch type: Sandy beach, paid entrance during summer season
Launch location: N44-29.601, W073-49.494
Facilities at launch: Rest rooms and campground
Wind exposure: Exposed to west and southwest wind

In the spring, I've been driven off this pond by swelling whitecaps. In the fall, I've been chased by a gray squall that turned the calm water into hail-thrashed turmoil in minutes. And other days, my kayak has cut across the mirror-still surface, my wake the only ripple during a 3-hour paddle.

This voyage begins at the Taylor Pond State Campsite. During the summer season, you'll have to pay a day-use fee. It's worth it. This pond is undeveloped, an Adirondack gem surrounded by state-owned wilderness.

From the launch, turn away from the earthen dam that blocks the east end of the pond and head west. You'll notice that the shore of the pond is littered with round boulders, some quite large. In several places near the shore, including the launch beach, boulders are submerged just below the surface.

Although this paddle does follow the shore, don't follow it too closely and keep an eye out for rocks. It can be startling to paddle full-steam ahead onto one of these big gray boulders.

At about 0.4 miles, having left the launch and small campground astern, you'll pass a couple of sharp points and deep bays, edged with boulders, birches and stumps of large drowned trees. You may also begin to see signs of beaver: scraps of chewed branches, shoreline trees with distinctive gnaw marks.

So, at 0.9 miles, you won't be surprised to pass a large beaver house, tucked into the shore. In some ways, Taylor Pond feels like an overgrown beaver pond: a smaller pond that was flooded to be much bigger.

All this time you have been paddling out of an elongated channel that leads to the main body of the pond. This southeast leg of the pond is pinched to its narrowest point about 1 mile into the trip. Continue into the main body of the lake, staying near the north (right) shore and rounding the final point that opens the full pond, an eroded peninsula topped by a large boulder, at 1.3 miles.

Now turn to the north and east, with the rocky cliffs of Silver Lake Mountain visible ahead. Continue to follow the shore toward the two outlet streams that leave the pond's northeast corner. The first of these outlets is shallow, protected by a small bar of sand and rocks. Pass briefly into this outlet at 1.9 miles.

The next outlet, sheltered by a low grassy island, begins at the far northern end of the pond at about 2 miles. This is a gorgeous spot: a deep, river-like bay where the forested shores seem to crowd in, the water still and glassy, Silver Lake Mountain looking down from the northeast and Catamount Mountain away on the southwest.

Deep in the inlet, round a large beaver lodge at 2.2 miles and turn back to the southwest. You could explore deeper into this magical place, but the main body of Taylor Pond awaits, with another inlet and a good

Photo/Jack Downs

A large beaver lodge dominates the northeast outlet of the main body of Taylor Pond.

pullout at the far end.

Exit the inlet at about 2.4 miles into the trip. Turn to the west and continue the counterclockwise circumnavigation. In some ways it feels like the paddle has just begun. It's time to settle in for a 2-mile pull along the somewhat straighter north shore, Douglas Mountain on your right, Catamount across the pond to the left. Occasional shallow bays open. Pass a lean-to at 3.45 miles, one of the few signs of civilization in this paddle. Even the walking path that circles this pond is usually invisible from the water.

As the west end of the pond approaches, the shoreline hugs closer to a steep mountain ridge and loses its regularity. Instead, the pond is edged with a series of jagged bays, studded with jumbled boulders. Ahead is the mountain pass where streams feed the pond.

Opposite a lean-to at 4.4 miles is a small rocky island. Coast through the shallow passage between island and shore to reach a narrow inlet that ends at a beaver dam 4.6 miles into the trip.

Continuing along the shore, turning now to the west, round a sandy shallows at the furthest end of the pond and paddle to the deeper inlet at the very southwest corner. At 5.2 miles this inlet, wider and stream-like, ends in another beaver dam. Watch out for submerged rocks. Nearby, a sandy beach clinging to the bouldered shore makes a convenient pullout, a good place to stretch your legs and admire the spectacular views before the long pull to the northeast.

This whole southwest end of Taylor Pond has a kind of natural magic: rugged bays, inlets, beaver dams, and an island to explore. And, like isolated spots on the eastern corners of the pond, there are small sand beaches here.

Back in the kayak and paddling east, leaving the bays and inlets behind, the shoreline again becomes more regular. Catamount Mountain towers over the pond here, making the shore much steeper, mountain streams tumbling down in places. In the northeast the vast series of ridges and cliffs that make up Silver Lake Mountain are now fully visible.

Continuing to paddle – it is more than 3 miles back to the launch, so this is no time to linger – take a glance over to the nearly parallel northern shore. Taylor Pond begins to feel like a huge rectangle that has been pulled and stretched at the corners. The northeastern corner, where we launched, has been yanked the hardest, nearly becoming its own 1-mile-long pond. Reach the entrance to this more sheltered portion of the pond at about 7 miles into the trip.

To complete the circumnavigation, follow the shore to the south and east. With Catamount Mountain now passing astern, the shoreline becomes lower and more beaver-dam like. This is again a region of submerged boulders. Pass the man-made earthen dam that controls the pond level at 8.4 miles. Return to the launch at 8.5 miles.

SIDE TRIPS/VARIATIONS

-- In my experience, Taylor Pond is a wind magnet, a weather channel between mountains. If the weather is uncertain when you launch, or if you are looking for a less strenuous paddle, stay in the more sheltered eastern end of the pond. A circle around this large bay will measure about 2.5 miles.

-- This trip can be expanded with longer explores into

the inlets and outlets. Or turn it into an overnight by reserving one of the handful of primitive campsites near the pond's beautiful western end.

-- After a paddle, why not give your legs a little exercise. A foot trail starting near the launch site encircles the pond, a route longer than this 8.5-mile paddle. Or take a hike up Silver Lake Mountain. The trailhead is just off Silver Lake Road, 1.7 miles north of the Taylor Pond State Campground entrance.

DRIVING DIRECTIONS

From the north on Route 3, turn south onto the Silver Lake Road in the hamlet of Clayburg. This intersection is about 3.5 miles west of Redford and about 5 miles east of the·Clinton/Franklin county line. At about 5.7 miles you will reach a stop sign. Continue on Silver Lake Road, turning right, and passing Silver Lake about 0.2 miles further. The entrance to Taylor Pond State Campsite is about 2.7 miles from this stop sign on the right.

From the south on Route 9N, drive to the center of AuSable Forks. Leave Route 9N where it intersects with Main Street adjacent to a Stewarts Shop. Take Main Street a short distance to the north. At the first stop sign, turn left. This road becomes Silver Lake Road. Pass through the hamlet of Black Brook. The entrance to Taylor Pond State Campsite is about 9.7 miles from AuSable Forks. Look for the driveway on the left.

TRIP NOTES

TRIP NOTES

_____

_____

_____

_____

_____

_____

_____

_____

_____

_____

_____

_____

_____

_____

_____

_____

_____

_____

_____

_____

_____

_____

_____

The Two Mouths of the Ausable

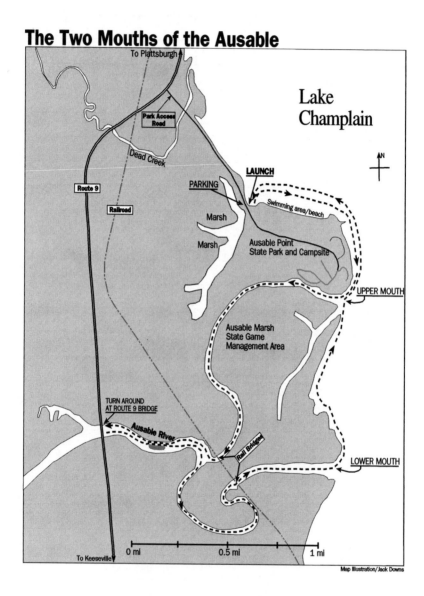

Map Illustration/Jack Downs

The Ausable River
A River with Two Mouths

A roundtrip river paddle starting and ending in Lake Champlain

NARRATIVE

River trips are usually one-way paddles. Upstream, then downstream, with the moving water providing all the variety a paddler needs. But the Ausable, with its two distinct mouths, opening wide around a huge sandy marsh, offers a rare river round-trip.

But first, a note of caution: This paddle begins and ends in Lake Champlain, which adds interest and complication.

Even though the lake portion of this paddle grips the shoreline, wind and waves are an issue. I recommend you avoid the passage around Ausable Point with a south wind of any magnitude. If the wind is a problem, look to the variations at the bottom of this narrative for some alternatives to an open-lake paddle.

Photo/Jack Downs

This narrow finger of sand separates AuSable Point beach from the true end of the point and the mouths of the Ausable River.

TRIP STATS
Rating: Moderate to Difficult
Time: 2.5 to 3 hours
Distance: 7.25 miles
Launch type: Sandy beach
Launch GPS location: N44-34.360, W073-25.965
Facilities at launch: None. However, launch is at the entrance for a state part where, for a daily fee during the park season, you can use all facilities.
Wind exposure: Exposed to a variety of winds. Use caution in windy conditions.

From the sandy launch area paddle to the southeast, paralleling Ausable Point State Beach. Stay well away from the swimming area. You will round a stone jetty at about 0.6 miles. The water shallows here, a hazard to larger boats. Although you can ignore the navigation buoys far off this point, give the jetty some leeway. Depending on the lake level, submerged rocks near the end of the structure can be close to the surface.

Now heading south, paddling parallel to the timber-reinforced head of the point, you will quickly see the difficulty a south or southeast wind can cause here. To the east and south lies the Broad Lake, miles of water stretch out to Vermont in the east and Crown Point in the south. Even on a quiet day the lake here may be a bit jumbled and uncomfortable, with wakes and waves bouncing off the point. With a strong wind, this portion of the paddle can be difficult for all but seasoned open-water paddlers equipped with sturdy sea kayaks.

Follow the shore, which becomes lower and turns

briefly to sand beach, around this southeastern tip of
Ausable Point and turn into the mouth of the Ausable at
about 1 mile into the trip. There appear to be two
passages here. Stay to the right, the north route is the true
mouth. The opening to the left dead-ends in the marsh.

Within about a half mile the impact of the lake is lost,
the campsites that had dotted the northern shore near the
lake are gone, the river turns glassy calm and wind and
waves are forgotten.

This is the prosaically named Upper Mouth of the
Ausable, a broad river, deep and dark. The current
should be slow, checking forward progress by only 1
mph or so. Quicker current means rain has swollen this
river and you should postpone your trip. Do not continue
if the current is at all difficult.

Hardwoods crowd close to the shore, overhanging it,
jungle-like. Ferns gather on the banks. Herons, ducks and
cormorants fish here. The air is alive with birdsongs.

Huge trunks protrude from the water here and there:
trees that have toppled and drowned. The sounds of the
State Park, the bustle of Route 9, seem a distant memory.
It would only take the addition of oppressive heat and an
equatorial sun to make this feel like a trip to the heart of
darkness.

The river makes a slow turn to the south, and then
back to the west, crossing under a railroad bridge at 2.5
miles.

This is where the river splits into upper and lower
mouths. As a variation, you may turn to the left here,
scooting downstream into the lower mouth, shortcutting
the trip and avoiding about 1.2 miles of paddling. A
description of that path follows later.

The main body of the river continues to the right, still

Photo/Jack Downs

The Upper Mouth of the Ausable River is tree-lined and
nearly tropical.

wide but gradually shallowing. Ahead is a long, narrow
island in midstream. The northern shore is an eroded sandy
bank pockmarked with swallow abodes. The current here
picks up slightly. If the water is low in extended dry
weather you may find navigation a bit difficult. The river
passes under the Route 9 highway bridge at 3.1 miles.

From a sandy pullout on the southern shore at the
bridge you can hear both the whine of the cars speeding
overhead, and the chattering rapids not far upstream.
This is a good place to take a break and then turn,
beginning downstream paddle.

By the clock, with the downstream flow speeding you
along, this is close to a halfway point. However,
measured on a map, you'll see that the Route 9 bridge
marks about 3.1 miles of a 7.25-mile trip.

Coasting downstream with the current, the railroad
bridge approaches quickly. Here, do not pass under the
bridge. Instead, turn to the right and start toward the
Lower Mouth of the Ausable. But use caution; the current
accelerates briefly where the river splits and narrows.

This southern branch of the river makes a dramatic
swing to the west and south, gradually widening and
slowing. At 4.3 miles the flow passes a small inlet and
butts up against a sandy, pine-covered headland to the
south, the first true high ground of the trip. Here, I watch
a whitetail doe skitter up the bank.

The loop twists back on itself, making a final sharp
turn to the west and running under a second railroad
bridge at about 4.9 miles. Within a hundred yards the
lake is visible at the end of a long, wide, straight stretch
that leads to the Lower Mouth at 5.5 miles.

The transition from river to lake here is sudden and
surprising. Riverbanks give way and the broad lake

opens before you.

Turn to the north (left) and follow the shore. If you stray further into the lake here you may be forced out quite a distance by the many sandbars at the mouth. This is definitely somewhere you don't want to paddle with a strong south or east wind pushing you into the shore. On the other hand, if the weather is calm and warm you may want to pause for some rest and sun on the long sand beach that leads to the Upper Mouth.

It is nearly a mile from the Lower Mouth to the Upper Mouth. Plan on about another mile to loop around Ausable Point and past the State Beach, tracing this paddle backwards. Mileage back to the launch site is 7.25 miles.

SIDE TRIPS/VARIATIONS

-- If you arrive for a paddle at Ausable Point and find a strong wind from the south or east you may want to change your destination. More than once I've put in at the launch site, paddled north along the beach only to stick my kayak bow around the stone jetty and turn back, with large waves rolling up from the south.

Instead, try Dead Creek, a stream that flows to the lake just to the west of the launch site. This is one of several Lake Champlain tributaries with this somber name.

To find it, paddle straight out from the launch site, making a wide turn to the west (left) around reed beds and sandbars. In the corner of this bay you'll see a narrow but deep inlet, sided by heavy reed banks. Follow it in and under the park access road. The stream is navigable for a few hundred yards ahead.

-- To avoid wind from the north, or to shorten this paddle slightly, enter the park and drive to the designated small-boat launch beach near the northwest corner of the parking lot. From here, launching near the stone jetty that is described in the narrative, the round trip is shortened by about a mile.

DRIVING DIRECTIONS

The entrance road to the Ausable Point State Beach leaves Route 9 about 7.5 miles south of the City of Plattsburgh and 4.5 miles north of Ausable Chasm.

From the north, drive south on Route 9 from Plattsburgh, watching for the Peru Boat Launch. The well-marked Ausable Point State Beach entrance is about 2.7 miles further south on the left.

From the south, driving north on Route 9, watch for the intersection of Bear Swamp Road (Route 442). The turn for the State Beach is 0.5 miles ahead on the right. By the way, Bear Swamp Road leads to Exit 35 of the Adirondack Northway (Route 87).

There is a small parking area on the right about 0.5 miles down the State Beach access road from Route 9. The launch area is across the road on the left, a sandy beach opening onto marsh. Don't mistakenly launch on the right (south) side of the access road. The marsh here is enclosed and there is little room to paddle.

If you choose to launch from the stone jetty or to use the swimming area you must continue on the access road to the park toll both, paying a fee during the camping season.

TRIP NOTES

_____

_____

_____

_____

TRIP NOTES

_____

_____

_____

_____

_____

_____

_____

_____

_____

_____

_____

_____

_____

_____

_____

_____

_____

_____

_____

_____

_____

_____

_____

_____

_____

Rouses Point

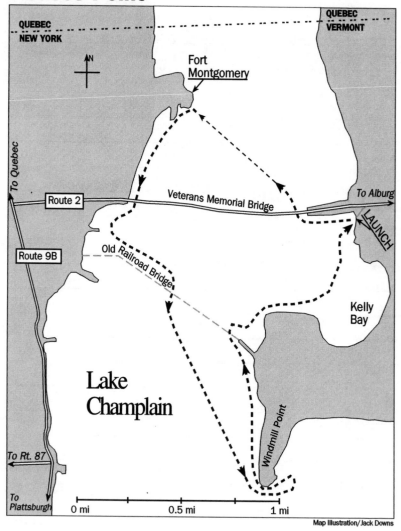

QUEBEC
VERMONT

QUEBEC
NEW YORK

N

Fort
Montgomery

To Quebec

Route 2

Veterans Memorial Bridge

To Alburg

LAUNCH

Route 9B

Old Railroad Bridge

Kelly
Bay

Lake
Champlain

Windmill Point

To Rt. 87

To
Plattsburgh

0 mi   0.5 mi   1 mi

Map Illustration/Jack Downs

Rouses Point
Paddling on the Border

A Lake Champlain Fort and Lighthouse

NARRATIVE

A historic fort, a huge bridge and a recently relit lighthouse. Not only is this a busy trip, packing all these features and more into 4 miles, our path crosses a busy waterway: the narrow channel at the north end of Lake Champlain.

Begin this paddle at a boat launch on the south side of the Vermont end of the Korean Veterans Memorial Bridge. Although this is a state-run concrete launch, it is geared for small boats and sided with gravel.

From this well-sheltered start, paddle west along the causeway that links the bridge to the Vermont shore. Kelly Bay opens on the south. Turn north (right) as the bridge leaves the shore, paddling under the span at 0.4 miles.

If there is a wind blowing, you will feel it here. Like

Photo/Gerianne Wright

The author paddles near the boat launch on the Vermont side of the Korean Veterans Memorial Bridge. The launch area is well-sheltered.

TRIP STATS
Rating: Moderate to difficult
Total distance: 4.75 miles
Approximate trip time: 1.5 to 2 hours
Launch GPS Location: 44-59.927, 073-19.900
Launch type: Concrete boat launch
Facilities at launch: Portable rest rooms
Wind Exposure: Vulnerable to south and north winds.

---

many Lake Champlain trips, this paddle is vulnerable to a south wind. Consider the Kelly Bay variation mentioned below if the channel appears choppy.

As you cross under the massive bridge, Fort Montgomery becomes visible across the lake. Head for it, but use care crossing the boating lane. This can be a hectic waterway, with oversized cabin cruisers, luxury sailboats and weekend speedboaters streaming to and from the Canada/U.S. border, churning up large wakes. Reach the fort at 0.7 miles into the trip.

Fort Montgomery has a fascinating history. Much newer than Fort Ticonderoga in the south, Fort Montgomery was built just after the War of 1812 by a young nation that feared yet another invasion from the north. But the builders were embarrassed to find that the fort was constructed on the wrong side of the border. Although a treaty later yielded the land to the United States, the structure never lost the nickname Fort Blunder.

But that wasn't the only blunder. As it turned out, waterborne invasion from the north was never again a threat. And military advances made massive stone forts obsolete before the construction here was finished. So the fort was abandoned. The walls were raided for stone, the interiors looted of anything valuable.

The fort is now on private land, posted against trespassing. Still, to paddle near these towering stone walls is impressive; to imagine giant cannons pointing from the enclosures is awe-inspiring.

Although Fort Blunder is now on our side of the border, the dividing line between the two nations remains close. Paddle just a couple hundred yards to the north and you will be in Canada.

Instead, turn to the south and head toward the bridge, staying on the west side of the boating channel. From this perspective, the span seems to snake across the lake. The shore here is marshy, quiet and undeveloped. Pass under the west end of the bridge at 1.6 miles.

A marina opens on the west shore here with the Village of Rouses Point behind. Weave through these busy waters carefully, heading for the opening in the line of wooden pilings ahead. This is an abandoned and partly demolished railroad bridge. Pass through the narrow opening at 2 miles into the trip, watching for boat traffic.

From here, look across to the Vermont shore in the southeast and head for a dominant point ahead. This is Windmill Point, made distinctive by its lighthouse, recently restored and relit. The metal tower that once held the automated navigation light still stands.

It's impossible not to compare this paddle to the Ticonderoga trip. Both pass by forts. Both travel portions of the lake that are narrow and river-like. But at Ticonderoga, the lake twists around Mount Independence and is sheltered by mountains to the west. Here, at Rouses Point, there are no mountains and little

Photo/Gerianne Wright

The historic Fort Montgomery looms on the New York shore of Lake Champlain just north of Rouses Point. This narrow channel was once of military significance.

shelter. The lake shoots straight to the north where it turns into the Richeleau River.

Reach the lighthouse at 3 miles and scoot a short distance to the south, rounding the point to find a sheltered place to take a breather. Gray rock ledge squeezes close to the surface here. After a rest, gazing at the Green Mountains to the east, turn back toward the bridge and begin the northward trip.

However, there is an obstacle ahead. Here, on the Vermont shore, the railroad bridge ends in a causeway made of jumbled slabs of white quarry waste. They protrude from the lake like huge, irregular cemetery monuments. Midway along this causeway is a break in the rocks and a small beach where you can pull out and explore. Reach it at 3.77 miles.

Back in the water, round the end of this causeway at 3.86 miles. This may be the trickiest part of the paddle. The piles that held up this end of the tracks are still here, barely submerged. If the lake is quiet, it isn't hard to slip between or glide over the piles, a kind of submerged forest. But if the lake level is low, or if waves are washing through the opening, you will have to paddle back to the main channel, adding about 0.5 miles to the trip.

Leaving the causeway behind, Kelley Bay opens on the east (right). Cut across it, heading toward the base of the bridge and back to the boat launch at 4.75 miles.

SIDE TRIPS/VARIATIONS

--If the wind is blowing, leave the open-water paddle for another day and explore Kelley Bay instead. Just to the south of the Vermont end of the Korean Veterans Memorial Bridge, this sheltered spot includes an island and forested shoreline.

-- Want to make this an international paddle? The border is within easy paddling distance from Fort Montgomery. The Canadian Customs dock is just north of the fort. The U.S. Customs dock is just south of the bridge. Both are on the west side of the lake. Even kayaks and canoes need to stop and report.

However, because the stretch of lake just north of the border isn't too interesting, you may want to keep your boat on the car and cross the border on land, driving to one of several launches along the Richeleau River just to the north.

DRIVING DIRECTIONS

From the intersection of Routes 9 and 11 in Rouses Point drive north about 1 mile to the New York/Vermont bridge. Look for the signs for Route 2. Cross the bridge. The launch is on Vermont shore on the south side (right) of the foot of the bridge. Distance from intersection of Routes 9 and 11 is about 3 miles.

TRIP NOTES

TRIP NOTES

TRIP NOTES

Crab Island

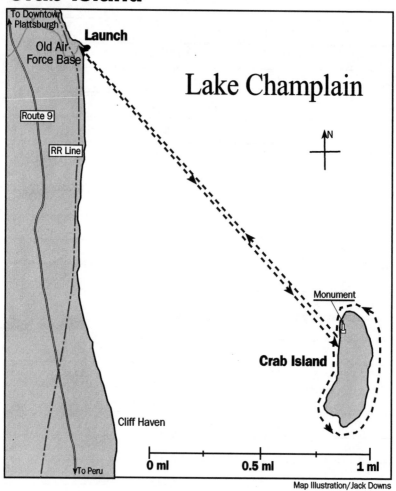

To Downtown Plattsburgh

Launch

Old Air Force Base

Lake Champlain

Route 9

RR Line

N

Monument

Crab Island

Cliff Haven

To Peru

0 ml   0.5 ml   1 ml

Map Illustration/Jack Downs

Crab Island
Round the Island from Sailor's Beach

A Lake Champlain Paddle in Plattsburgh Bay

NARRATIVE

Driving through the former Plattsburgh Air Force Base to reach the starting point for this paddle should put you in a military frame of mind. Pause on the steep railroad bridge that leads to the lake for a battlefield panorama of Plattsburgh Bay, a view fit for an admiral.

Center stage is Crab Island, a silent witness to military history. During the War of Independence and the War of 1812 naval fleets maneuvered these waters. With cannon and saber, brave Americans defended our nation from the British. War dead of both nations are buried on Crab Island.

Crab Island's position, once strategic, is now picturesque: close enough for an easy daytrip; far enough

Photo/Jack Downs

The Crab Island Monument honors the island's military
history.

TRIP STATS
Rating: Moderate to Difficult
Distance from beach to island, bearing almost directly south, 1.7 miles
Total distance, including turn around island: 4.6 miles
Total paddling time: 1:15 to 1:45
Launch GPS location: N44-40.881, W073-26.488
Launch type: Both concrete launch and sandy beach available
Facilities at launch: None
Wind: Exposed to a variety of winds. Use caution.

away to be its own isolated little world.

Begin at Sailor's Beach, once an active recreation area for Plattsburgh Air Force Base, now an informal boat launch favored by kayakers and other small boaters. The parking area is paved. You can launch from the somewhat stony sand beach on the south, or the concrete boat ramp at the north.

From here, head almost due south. You'll have no problem finding the island, but be warned, it's not as close as it looks.

The crossing, about 1.7 miles, is exposed to the wind and has the potential for waves on all but the calmest days. On popular summer weekends boat traffic and wakes can be a problem. However, the channel is wide enough to give everyone the room they need.

As the island approaches – like most islands do, seeming to recede and then looming large with only a few hundred yards to go – you'll see the monument: a simple obelisk. Aim for this marker and the recently restored flagpole nearby.

The shore here is a combination of broken stone and

Photo/Jack Downs

Crab Island's rocky shore can make landing a large boat difficult. However, canoes and kayaks, paddled carefully, can beach safely.

ledge. But you won't find anywhere much better to land – Crab Island isn't know for sandy beaches. If you plan to explore the island on foot, this is a good place to start. But beware of poison ivy. You may want to bring a pair of long pants and good shoes for protection. No camping is allowed.

When viewing the monument, respect is called for. On Memorial Day, visitors bring flowers to honor the war dead buried in lost graves here. The dead are also honored on days commemorating battles of the War of Independence and the War of 1812.

Turning to the southwest, begin a counterclockwise loop around the island. From here you'll now get a view of Valcour Island to the southwest. It quickly becomes obvious how much larger Valcour, 1,100 acres, is than Crab, 40 acres. Looking down on the scene, castle-like on a high bluff on the New York shore to the south, is Clinton Community College, which had once been the Hotel Champlain in the 1800s and early 1900s.

Continuing around the rugged island, paddle past broken rock and ledges with a few abandoned and decrepit concrete slabs. Rounding the southwestern tip of the island reveals a small bay and, on the south shore, continued broken rock. Watch for stately herons, standing still on the gray rock. You'll have to look carefully; their camouflage is almost perfect here.

On one recent trip – Memorial Day, appropriately – the Vermont-facing shore was busy with birds. I paddled through a cloud of swallows darting bat-like inches from the water, feeding on some kind of insect hatch. Several herons glided past, a number of ducks of unusual color fished in the shallows while cormorants claimed the deeper water. And a mysterious pair of loons dove off the northeast point of the island.

Paddling east along this shore Cumberland Head becomes visible away to the north. This bulky point shelters the northwest side of Plattsburgh Bay. Away on your east is Vermont, the hazy Green Mountains on the horizon. Continue around the eastern tip of the island, reaching the monument again at about 1.2 miles.

With your back to the monument, looking across the wide channel, you may have a moment of confusion. Where are Sailor's Beach and the boat launch? If you have a compass, take a bearing just to the west of north. Otherwise, look for the Plattsburgh Harbor Marina to the north, scan a bit to the west and south until you make out a couple of large brick buildings. Head for these.

Unless the wind has picked up to add some interest to the return crossing, you should find it uneventful. Enjoy the rhythm of the paddling and the quiet of the open water. Maybe you will get lucky and see a freight train chugging along the nearby Canadian Pacific line. Return to Sailor's Beach at 4.6 miles.

VARIATIONS/SIDE PADDLES

Sailor's Beach is a good jumping off place for a number of possible side trips.

-- Follow the lake shore north and you can explore Plattsburgh Harbor Marina, the mouth of the Saranac River, Wilcox Dock and the long stretch of beach at the head of the bay that includes the Plattsburgh City Beach and Cumberland Bay State Park.

-- Follow the shore south and you'll pass by the old Plattsburgh Air Force Base fuel docks – barges used to deliver jet fuel here – Cliff Haven and Bluff Point.

-- Because Sailor's Beach is somewhat exposed to a

south wind and the waves that come with it, this is a good place to practice wave skills close to shore on a windy day.

DRIVING DIRECTIONS

To reach the launch, begin at the main entrance to the former Plattsburgh Air Force Base: the intersection of Route 9 and New York Avenue, near the southern boundary of the City of Plattsburgh. Approaching from the south on Route 9 this intersection is about 4.4 miles from the Peru Boat Launch. From the north, it is about 1.2 miles from the bridge where Route 9 crosses the Saranac River in the heart of downtown Plattsburgh. Also at this intersection are Skyway Shopping Center and a small park with static displays of Air Force craft.

Turn east onto New York Avenue, driving into what is still called the Old Base. Very soon you'll see Ohio Avenue East on your right. Take this turn. The signs for Ohio Avenue veer off, but don't follow them. Stay on this road. Now, only 0.3 miles from the base entrance, you will approach the railroad tracks and see a narrow bridge that crosses the tracks toward the lake. Take this turn, watching for traffic on the one-lane bridge and the hairpin turn that follows it. The launch is just ahead, a total of 0.5 miles from the intersection of Route 9 and New York Avenue.

TRIP NOTES

_____

_____

_____

_____

TRIP NOTES

TRIP NOTES

Valcour Island

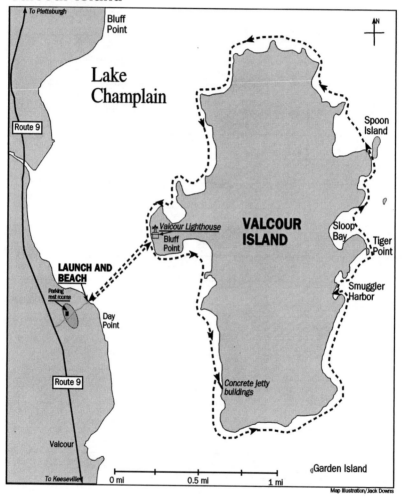

Map Illustration/Jack Downs

Valcour Island
Round the Island
from Peru Boat Launch

Lake Champlain's Historic Gem

NARRATIVE

Valcour Island is big in lots of ways: the island looms large in American naval history; there are enough bays, beaches and cliffs here to fill a much larger land mass; and at 4 miles long and a mile wide, Valcour is literally bigger than most other Lake Champlain islands.

Although Valcour gets big marks on the recreation scale, the effort you need to get there is relatively small. The island is just a bit more than a half-mile from one of the lake's busiest access points.

It is from the Peru Boat Launch that this trip begins. This large state-run launch is often crowded, so you may want to park in the lot and carry your kayak or canoe to the rocky beach just to the north of the launch. Take care on the somewhat dilapidated stone and concrete steps.

Photo/Jack Downs

This concrete jetty leads to stone steps and some of the few buildings that remain on the island.

TRIP STATS
Rating: Moderate to difficult
Total distance: 7 miles
Approximate trip time: 2.5 to 3 hours
Launch GPS Location: 44-37.178, 073-26.616
Launch type: Free concrete boat launch with rocky beach available
Facilities at launch: Rest rooms
Wind Exposure: Vulnerable to south or north wind.

From here the island is obvious: it dominates the view. Carefully wind your way through the shallows, watching for rocks close to the surface, and then head east, making for the Valcour Lighthouse, high on a bluff dead ahead.

As you leave the protection of the bay, entering the narrow channel between Valcour Island and the mainland, make an honest assessment of the wind and waves. Weather here should be a warning: heed it. In my experience, even a moderate south wind can build swelling waves here, seemingly amplified by the narrowing channel to become almost ocean-like. If the wind is blowing, this is a good place to turn back.

Continue across the channel, keeping an eye out for motorboats leaving and returning from the boat launch. The crossing provides a superb view of the Valcour Lighthouse with its distinctive architecture. The light is actually carried by a higher metal tower nearby. Crab Island is visible to the north, as are the red roofs of Clinton Community College, high on Bluff Point.

Finish the crossing at 0.6 mile. Resting close to the rock cliffs the lighthouse is now invisible, perched out of view overhead. There is nowhere to pull out here.

However, there are deep bays with sand beaches on either side of this headland where you can begin an explore of the island and walk to a closer view of the lighthouse.

Turn to the south (right), beginning a counterclockwise circumnavigation of the island. Much of this south end of the island is ledge and cliff, with cedars and wiry pines clinging to rock outcroppings.

At 0.85 miles, cross the mouth of the first of numerous deep bays that make this island such a favorite among sailors. It's not unusual to see several large sailboats moored in these sheltered coves. Motorboaters, canoers and kayakers also come here for the sand beaches and wilderness.

Hundreds of years ago these same bays sheltered the fledgling American Navy. With Benedict Arnold in command they hid here and surprised a much larger and more powerful British fleet on Oct. 11, 1776. The Americans, upwind and with the element of surprise, foiled the British invasion plans. War dead from both fleets are likely still buried on the island.

At 1.68 miles into the trip pass a concrete jetty that leads to stone stairs. This is access to some of the remaining buildings in what is mostly wild forest. Although Valcour is largely remembered for its military history, at various times it was the home to farms, a luxury lodge and an early utopian community. This is another good place to beach the boat and explore.

But please treat Valcour Island gently. This historic gem has suffered from recreational overuse. Camp only with permission, and only at designated campsites. Make no fires, except in designated firepits.

Also visible early in the trip around Valcour are small numbered signs. These are the markers — white numbers on a blue background — for state-monitored campsites that dot the shore. This is primitive camping: expect no showers or shopping here. For camping reservations contact the State Department of Environmental Conservation.

Continuing south, round the southwestern tip of the island at 1.8 miles. Here, the gray rock cliffs rear higher, witness to brutal storms that smash this shore. Broken boulders wrenched from the face lie smashed at the foot of the headland. Floating calmly at the base of the cliff on a warm August afternoon it is sobering to imagine the fury of a November gale, the south wind screaming across the broad lake, lashing this impressive promontory.

Garden Island, tiny, rectangular and rocky, sits just off this rugged southern shore. Sometimes also called Gunboat Island, this lonely rock can be mistaken as a small ship from shore.

Continuing around the southern tip of the island, Vermont's Green Mountains come into view. At about 2.3 miles into the trip pass a rocky beach. A series of small bays and points follow and the shore begins to turn to the northeast.

At 2.65 miles the east side of the island opens in a large low, ledge-shored bay. There is little traffic here. The busy boat launch is far away now. Herons fish on the shore. Duck families float by.

What seems like one huge bay though is really two. Seemingly hidden, Smuggler's Harbor opens at 3.1 miles, cutting sharply into the island to the south and west. Paddle deep into this cove and you'll find a sandy beach and a fenced memorial to the captain and crew of the Nomad, a World War I vessel. This is a great place to stop, have lunch, stretch your legs or have a swim.

It seems that an island bounds Smuggler's Harbor on

the north. Really, this is Tiger Point, narrowly connected to Valcour. Round it and you will see two islands ahead with Cumberland Head distant between them. Another deep bay, this one called Sloop Cove, opens at 3.6 miles.

Pass the first island and approach the second, Spoon Island, a distinctly shaped, cliff-walled mass that almost touches Valcour. Carefully thread the shallows between the Spoon and Valcour at 4.1 miles into the trip, opening Spoon Bay, one of a continuing series of deep bays, many footed with sandy beaches.

After Spoon Bay the shore begins to gradually turn to the northeast. The shoreline now is much lower and the points that separate the bays are low protrusions of tumbled rock and grass.

Ahead, Crab Island is nearing. But it looks closer than it is. The true distance is about 1.5 miles. That's a longer open-water paddle than I'd want to take on more than 4 miles into a trip.

At 4.8 miles, reach the northern most tip of Valcour Island. The water here is shallow, with much broken rock close to the surface. These bays protect some of the prettiest beaches on the island. Clinton Community College again is visible high on Bluff Point. Plattsburgh Bay opens to the north. Continuing to paddle, the shoreline turns first to the west and then the southwest. The Adirondacks are massive shadows to the west and south.

Now heading south, leaving Bluff Point and Crab Island behind, the central headland that supports the lighthouse looms nearer. At 6.2 miles into the trip the last bay before the lighthouse opens. Passing this bay, the gray cliffs quickly rise up again. Reach the cliff face underneath the lighthouse at 6.38 miles.

Turn now toward the Peru Boat Launch, visible

Photo/Jack Downs

A kayaker floats in Smuggler's Harbor on the west side of
Valcour Island.

directly across the channel to the west. Watching for boat traffic, wakes, and hoping that the winds have stayed calm, cross the channel to finish this paddle, landing at the launch at 7 miles.

SIDE TRIPS/VARIATIONS

-- Valcour Island provides all the variations you can want: hiking, camping and beach fun. It's easy to turn the short paddle from the launch to the island into a family adventure by stopping at the first beach you find and exploring, leaving the circumnavigation for another day. But again, please treat the island gently.

-- If wind is a problem, consider changing the direction of the circumnavigation.

-- If wind keeps you from crossing to Valcour Island you may want to explore the shoreline with its luxury lakeside homes and the nearby marina.

DRIVING DIRECTIONS

From the south on Route 9, the Peru Boat Launch is about 2.7 miles north of Ausable Point State Beach.

From the north on Route 9, the launch is about 1.7 miles south of the junction of Route 9 and New York Avenue. You can identify this intersection — entrance to the former Plattsburgh Air Force Base, by the warplanes displayed in a small park beside the road.

TRIP NOTES

_____

_____

_____

_____

TRIP NOTES

Schuyler Island

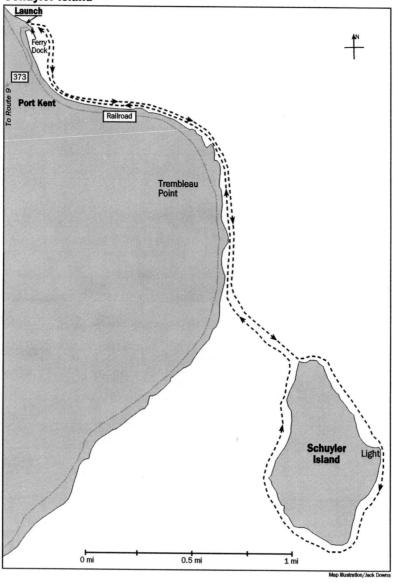

Map illustration/Jack Downs

Schuyler Island
Round the Island
from Port Kent

A Lake Champlain Paddle to a
Little-Visited Island

NARRATIVE

For many, Port Kent is a window on the lake. The ferry ride from here to Burlington is, for most non-boaters, one of the only times in their lives they'll spend an hour on the water.

But for me, an hour on the ferry is a tease. If riding on the ferry is being "on" the water, I long to be "in" it, feeling the liquid element through the thin skin of my kayak.

Launching from Port Kent is pleasant, with easy access to the public beach from a nearby parking lot. During the summer season, avoid the swimming area. Make sure to use the beach — just past the ferry ticket

A trip to Schuyler Islands begins at the beach near the Port Kent ferry landing.

TRIP STATS
Rating: Moderate to Difficult
Total distance: 6.6 miles
Total Time: 2-2.5 hours
Launch type: Sandy beach
Launch: N44-31.650, W73-24.315
Launch facilities: Water, food and rest rooms available
at ferry dock.
Wind exposure: Expect waves with wind. This paddle is
especially exposed to wind from the north and east.

booth — and not the small, steep tarmac boat launch you
pass on the way.

The beach is sheltered from all but an east wind.
Leaving the beach, turn to the southeast (right) and
round the ferry dock carefully, watching for boat traffic.
Head across this small bay, now somewhat more exposed
to wind.

A long sandy beach approaches on the base of the
rising headland here: Trembleau Point. However, paddle
a bit closer and the scene is not so inviting. Posted signs
dot the beach. Almost all the shoreline near Port Kent is
private property.

Follow the shoreline closely here, watching the sandy
beach give way to boulders, ledge and rock cliff at about
0.75 miles.

Keep an ear open for traffic on the Canadian Pacific
railroad line, high up on the rocky headland, paralleling
the lake. This lakeshore scenery adds a touch of beauty to
the Amtrak Adirondacker's NYC-to-Montreal route. Just
so, the sound of a passenger or freight train pounding
along the tracks overhead adds a startling but interesting

element to the paddling experience.

As you round Trembleau Point the lake opens dramatically. The skyline of Burlington is obvious in the east, seeming deceptively close, with the Green Mountains rising in the hazy distance beyond. Really, Burlington is almost 10 miles distant, a solid 3 hours of paddling for me. Not the sort of open-water trip to be taken lightly.

The long point sheltering Willsboro Bay is visible to the south. But directly in our path is Schuyler Island.

Depending on the wind direction and waves, you may veer from the shore and angle toward the island when it first becomes visible, or you may continue along the shoreline for a bit, cutting across the 0.5-mile channel between mainland and island a bit further to the south at its narrowest point. The shortest route, slanting off to reach the island when it first becomes visible, brings you to the island at about 2.2 miles. This angled crossing lengthens the open-water paddle to about 1 mile.

Reaching the north tip of Schuyler Island, the lake shallows dramatically. The approach is shallow and rock-strewn, a hazard to larger boats but easy for a carefully paddled kayak or canoe.

From landfall at the north tip, travel clockwise around the island, passing an automated navigation light at 2.9 miles, rounding the forested and bluff-like south end at 3.5 miles. Shelter is available in a small, broken-rock bay just around the island's rocky south end at about 3.8 miles.

Schuyler Island is state owned. Primitive camping is allowed on these 123 acres for registered groups. Historically, the island is noteworthy for a minor role in the October 1776 Battle of Lake Champlain. Here, fleeing

Photo/Jack Downs

The rocky shore of Trembleau Point near the Schuyler Island channel.

a stronger British fleet after remarkable success in conflict near Valcour Island, American commander Benedict Arnold allowed his men to rest. He scuttled three badly damaged vessels near the island before fleeing again in a running battle with the British.

Circumnavigation of the island takes about 2.2 miles. Return to the north end of the island at 4.35 miles into the trip.

The paddle back to Port Kent is a simple backtrack. However, covering the same route in reverse is not repetitive. Heading north and west opens a very different vista: luxury homes on Trembleau Point on your left, the ferry route running like a highway in the lake to your right, and the small marina at the ferry dock becoming visible as you round the point and head back to the beach, ending at about 6.6 miles.

VARIATIONS AND SIDE TRIPS

There are two obvious shoreline side trips from Port Kent.

-- After rounding Trembleau Point, you may decline the open-water crossing to Schuyler Island, instead paddling further to the south through Corlear Bay toward Port Douglas, a distance of about 2.5 miles.

-- As another alternative, especially if the wind is from the south, travel north from Port Kent, still paralleling the railroad line. Here, the shoreline is sandy, with several unposted and somewhat unkempt beaches that are obviously informal swimming areas. To the north you can see Ausable Point and the two mouths of the Ausable River. Here also the railroad is lower, closer to the water, traveling on a causeway that separates Lake Champlain from Wickham Marsh. From Port Kent to the large culvert that drains the marsh is about 1 mile.

DRIVING DIRECTIONS

To get to Port Kent, from the north or south, you must first take Route 9 and then turn onto Route 373. From the north the intersection of routes 9 and 373 is well to the south of Plattsburgh. You'll find the turn about 2.3 miles south of the Route 9 highway bridge over the Ausable River. From the south the intersection of routes 9 and 373 is 1.8 miles from the intersection of routes 9 and 9N in the Village of Keeseville. You'll know you are close when you see the sign for Ausable Chasm.

Once you reach Route 373 the launch is easy to find. Travel east about 3.2 miles from the intersection with Route 9. You'll know you're almost there when the lake becomes visible. Route 373 crosses a railroad track, turns sharply and the ferry dock is ahead. Go straight past the ferry area to the beach.

TRIP NOTES

TRIP NOTES

TRIP NOTES

TRIP NOTES

TRIP NOTES

TRIP NOTES